Praise for *Tragedy in the Commons*

"Disturbing tales of dys~~~~~~~~~~~~~~~~~~~~~~~~~~views
offer eye-opening insight into a system in deep malaise."
Elizabeth Renzetti, *The Globe and Mail*

"I learned a lot from this book and I've been covering politics my whole life." Kevin Newman, national broadcaster

"There's much to be learned from *Tragedy in the Commons*—it's a real page-turner, with informative writing and exciting stories. . . . *Tragedy in the Commons* is fascinating and well-researched. . . . It won't disappoint." *The Telegram*

"*Tragedy in the Commons* is a thoughtful analysis of what is broken in our democracy and a must-read for anyone concerned about Canada's politics. It's also a cogent and urgent reminder that the struggle to make our Parliament and our politics work falls not only to politicians, but to us all." Terry Fallis, author of *The Best Laid Plans*

"This important book draws on the personal experiences of former Members of Parliament to illustrate the growing central control of party leadership—in all major parties—and how this has distorted the democratic process. Offering useful suggestions to address the resulting alienation of voters from the political process, *Tragedy in the Commons* is mandatory reading for all MPs and Canadians." Michael Wilson, former Minister of Finance and Canadian Ambassador to the United States

"Canadians' participation in and respect for democracy are fundamental to maintaining a society of which we can be proud. Through the reflections of Members of Parliament, who have devoted themselves to public life, Loat and MacMillan give us insight into how far we have to travel, and how urgent is the cause." Amanda Lang, co-host of *The Lang & O'Leary Exchange* and author of *The Power of Why*

"[Loat and MacMillan have] done an excellent job, and published an engaging read out of powerful and unique source material. . . . I finished this book over a month ago and it's still rolling around in my mind. When voters go shopping, [they should] pick this up." *cpsrenewal* (blog)

"In every tragedy there is hope. Members of Parliament go to Ottawa hoping and promising to make a difference; but as these riveting revelations show, high priorities get lost too easily in the widening chasm between constituents, party leaders and good conscience. Is it any wonder Canadians feel disengaged from their hard-won democracy? Loat and MacMillan hope that pulling back the curtain will re-engage Canadians enough to keep our House of Commons from becoming a 'House of Cards.'" Isabel Bassett, former Member of Provincial Parliament

"A valuable study. . . . The first concerted effort to conduct exit interviews with retired and defeated parliamentarians." *Maclean's*

"An important book that aims to salvage a system that seems destined to remain as is: broken." *rabble.ca*

Alison Loat & Michael MacMillan

TRAGEDY
in the
COMMONS

Former Members of Parliament Speak Out
About Canada's Failing Democracy

VINTAGE CANADA

VINTAGE CANADA EDITION, 2015

Copyright © 2014 Alison Loat and Michael MacMillan

Published in Canada by Vintage Canada, a division of Random House of Canada Limited, a Penguin Random House Company, in 2015. Originally published in hardcover in Canada by Random House Canada, a division of Random House of Canada Limited, in 2014. Distributed in Canada by Random House of Canada Limited, Toronto.

Vintage Canada with colophon is a registered trademark.

www.penguinrandomhouse.ca

LIBRARY AND ARCHIVES CANADA CATALOGUING IN PUBLICATION

Loat, Alison, author
Tragedy in the Commons : former Members of Parliament speak out about Canada's failing democracy / Alison Loat and Michael MacMillan.

ISBN 978-0-307-36130-1
eBook ISBN 978-0-307-36131-8

1. Canada. Parliament. House of Commons. 2. Legislators—Canada. 3. Canada—Politics and government. I. MacMillan, Michael, author II. Title.

JL161.L63 2015   328.71'072   C2013-906318-8

Text design by Five Seventeen
Image credits: © Doug Armand/The Image Bank/Getty Images

Printed and bound in the United States of America

2 4 6 8 9 7 5 3 1

To our parents,
Mary and Iain MacMillan,
and Trish and Chris Loat

CONTENTS

"Let's start at the beginning. Can you talk a bit about how you got interested in public life?"

"I was a fairly normal kid, and playing football or hockey was a lot more important to me. I mean, I had walked in the civil rights marches, I was very interested in the Third World. I was very interested in the environment, which at that time was just beginning to be an issue. . . . But I really never had an interest in going into politics. I was going to the Third World. That was my ultimate aim, to go to the Third World, but I wanted to make money before I went. . . . And I suddenly, really very late in life, decided that I was going to run in public life. [A friend who was active in politics] came to see me to try to convince me to run. . . . And I said, 'I've got to think about it.' And he said to me, 'Don't think about it. If you do that, you will never run.' And you know, I said, 'That's probably good advice.' And I didn't think about it, and I ran."

In 2009 we founded Samara, a think tank dedicated to raising the level of political participation in Canada. We named it after the term used to describe the winged "helicopter" seed that falls from maple trees. As a symbol, it says to us that out of small ideas, big things can grow. Soon afterward, together with members of the Samara staff, we began travelling across the country to interview former Members of Parliament. We spent two or three hours with each MP, often in the comfort of their own homes and communities, and between that first year and 2013, we interviewed eighty men and women from all parts of the country. Some had left politics voluntarily, after short or long careers, while others were voted out of office. Taken together, they represented all five parties who sat in the 38th, 39th and 40th Parliaments (2004–11). We believe this to be the first large-scale, systematic series of exit interviews with former Members of Parliament in Canada or, for that matter, anywhere in the world.

When we embarked on this project, we hoped ten or fifteen former MPs might agree to speak with us. We were wrong. Nearly everyone we approached offered to meet and share their slice of history and advice. They gave generously of their time and ideas, often opening their homes to complete strangers, and we are grateful to them for the opportunity to hear their reflections on their service.

Why did we do it? We were searching for an answer to a complicated problem.

Canada is among the world's most successful democracies. Look at any international ranking of democracy, and we appear, almost without fail, near the top. *The Economist* Intelligence Unit's Democracy Index ranks the world's sovereign states by how democratic they are, and Canada has placed in the top ten since the index was first published in 2006. In 2012 we placed eighth, well ahead of the United States and the United

Kingdom. On Transparency International's 2012 Corruption Perceptions Index, we tied with the Netherlands as the ninth-least corrupt nation in the world. And in Freedom House's survey, Canada is deemed "free." Period. Top of the pile.

Yet these rankings are increasingly difficult to square with the growing sense among Canadians that the country's politics are not working quite as they should. For well over a generation, in election after election, voter turnout has declined, and millions of dollars in government and political party advertising have done little to arrest the decline. Political party membership is rare to non-existent in most parts of the country, and many who do join become disillusioned and cynical. Talk to campaign volunteers or candidates, and they'll tell you how hard it is to get citizens involved. When politicians knock, many people don't even answer the door, and if they do, they rarely want to talk policy and ideas.

Some may argue that this reluctance is in fact a sign of satisfaction with the status quo, but research does not bear that out. Canadians are becoming less happy with the way we are governed. For example, public opinion research commissioned by Samara in 2012 revealed that only 55 percent of Canadians were satisfied with the state of their democracy. Ten years earlier, when Canadians were asked the same question, the result was twenty points higher. Canadians face a great number of challenges today—environmental sustainability, economic prosperity, increasing rates of poverty, effective health care delivery, to name but a few. Most money that Canadians spend in these areas comes as a direct result of decisions made by our governments and politicians. Making the right decisions is critical to ensuring a continued high quality of life for all of us, whether we were born here or moved here from somewhere else.

In other countries, citizens risk their lives to have a voice in government and the ability to influence the decisions made in their own legislatures. They are motivated by a belief that democratic processes are better able than aristocracies, dictatorships or other governmental models to respond to the challenges facing their citizens. In Canada, we may have come to take our right to a functioning democracy for granted. Voting trends are but one indicator among many: Canadians are checking out of their democracy in droves.

So who is best positioned to help solve this problem? Who understands the system well enough to be able to identify what's driving that wedge between Canadians and their system of government, and where solutions might be found? And, when push comes to shove, who is most responsible for and often takes much of the blame for our lamentable state of affairs?

Members of Parliament.

We thought interviews with MPs would illuminate how Canada's democracy works, right at its front line. Conventional wisdom holds that the best ideas for improving an organization reside in the minds and experiences of those closest to it. What could be done to improve patient care in our hospitals? Talk to the doctors and nurses. Want to eliminate waste on the factory floor? Ask the line workers where changes could be made.

Current parliamentarians live and work in the thick of the action. But they are also busy and often governed by a partisan agenda. So in our search for answers, we thought *former* MPs—those who were out of the public eye and had gained perspective on their time in office—might have some answers.

WITH EVERY FEDERAL ELECTION in this country, more than 1,600 people are nominated as candidates to become one of the 308 who serve as Members of Parliament in Canada's House of Commons. (The number of our federal legislators was poised to rise to 338 in 2015.) These men and women vie to become a part of history, to be among the few citizens chosen by their communities to act as representatives to the rest of their country—to make important decisions on behalf of Canada, allocate billions of dollars, represent the country internationally and determine which problems the country will work to solve.

In these exit interviews, we asked the former parliamentarians to describe what brought them to public life. We inquired into their motives and their paths to politics. We asked how they spent their time in office. How did they interact with their constituents and civil society organizations? What did they view as their accomplishments in office? How did they work within their party? And what advice did they have for future MPs—and for Canadians themselves?

During the interviews, the former MPs were at times cagey, protective of themselves, their parties and their place in Canada's public life. But for the most part, they were open, helpful and forthcoming about their experiences and the problems they identified in the way our politics works. Many said the questions we posed were questions they'd never been asked before, or at least hadn't fully considered. Like us, they wanted to better understand and find solutions to Canadians' growing disengagement with and lack of trust in our elected leaders, as it is a disenchantment that many of the former parliamentarians also share. Our interviews together present a composite insider's portrait of the Green Chamber with implications that should both trouble and, we hope, motivate, all of us.

Tragedy in the Commons is also a snapshot of a specific time and place. The men and women we interviewed served in Parliament on average for ten and a half years, many when the Bloc Québécois, Reform Party and, later, Canadian Alliance and Conservative Party of Canada were rising to the status of important players on the national stage. Interviews with former Liberal members reflect their party's transition out of a long period of forming governments. Similarly, the new Conservative Party was undergoing its own transition, from outsider mavericks to prototypical insiders, from a party bent on reforming government to one that was forming government. Each of the participating MPs had served in at least one minority Parliament, and many of our early interviewees had the sense that the House of Commons had entered a period of perpetual minorities. (Obviously, they weren't clairvoyant.)

We approached this project as documentarians, reporting MPs' accounts of their feelings and beliefs. In some cases, their memories were no doubt coloured by the passage of time and affected by the lens through which they chose to interpret their own lives and experiences. Regardless, the ways in which they chose to remember themselves and the moments they chose to share with us often brought forward the most candid portrayals of how Canadian democracy really works.

These interviews also reflect views and problems that

are common to all parties and as old as the House of Commons itself. What one MP said about the Liberals or the Bloc in the past will likely also be true of the Conservatives or the NDP today. The same complaints about the Liberals after their long reign could also apply to Brian Mulroney's Tories in 1993, or probably to any long-serving governments in the future.

The problems illuminated in our exit interviews can seem intractable. One need only glance at Queen's University professor C.E.S. Franks's book *The Parliament of Canada* to grasp how long some of these problems have been around: "The themes of reform have not changed," Franks notes. "The same complaints of excessive partisanship, government domination, lack of influence of the private member and the need for improved committees and accountability, for a greater role for Parliament in policy-making, and for reform of the Senate continue despite the passage of time and the many changes that have been made." Franks's book sounds current; it was published in 1987.

AFTER REVIEWING MORE THAN four thousand pages of transcripts from our eighty interviews with MPs from across the political spectrum and every province, we were struck by the themes that prevailed throughout the interviews. Politicians frequently try to define themselves as opposites—Liberals versus Conservatives, men versus women, and Easterners versus Westerners. But what stood out for us was how much these MPs agreed with one another, particularly on points that together indicated a desperate need for solutions.

One of those common themes? The MPs liked to say they were not politicians. They told us they'd never planned to run for federal office. In fact, many articulated opposition to the political establishment as an important reason why they entered politics in the first place.

At the start of this introduction, we quoted an MP who professed that he never planned to run. That MP was the Right Honourable Paul Martin, Canada's minister of finance for nearly nine years and its prime minister for a little more than two. He was the son of an MP, himself a Cabinet minister and a leadership candidate. The younger Martin grew up travelling with his father to Ottawa, the UN and countless constituency events. Though he acknowledged his early and uncommon exposure to politics, even the former prime minister claimed he didn't think about being a politician until he was in his mid-forties, and even then only with the urging of others.

Once in office, many MPs continued to identify themselves as outsiders. Reflecting on MPs behaving badly in the House of Commons or in the media, most said they never engaged in *that sort* of behaviour themselves. And they're outsiders when they blame their parties, organizations of which they are actively a part, for forcing them to vote against their wishes—or against the desires of their constituents. And they're outsiders when imparting their most oft-stated advice, that to survive as an MP, one must stay true to oneself and not get caught up in the "Ottawa bubble" in which they were elected to serve. The persistence of the outsider narrative suggests an antipathy to political ambition so deeply ingrained in our society that even our politicians can't admit to having wanted to be in Parliament, and shun the moniker of politician.

A second theme that runs throughout the interviews is the extent to which each MP is managed by his or her political party. Most of these individuals came to Ottawa with experience as leaders in their communities. They had served on school boards, volunteered with community agencies, Rotary Clubs or Chambers of Commerce. They'd coached sports teams, coordinated local events and solved local problems. These are individuals with tremendous energy, persuasive power and abilities to get things done. They endured election campaigns and convinced thousands of voters to elect them. But even before they arrived in Ottawa—usually in the nomination process—they began to feel the controlling influence of their chosen party. After they left politics, this constricting influence nagged at them still. Although we didn't originally ask about party influence in the exit interviews, once we saw how much the MPs wished to discuss it, we had to ask.

These two themes are intertwined: MPs were reluctant to stand up for their profession as politicians, and opted instead to distance themselves from their "typical" peers. Simultaneously, many MPs professed to feeling discomfort when wearing their party sweaters; that is, when having to adhere fully to party discipline. Many chose to tell us about times they disagreed with their leaders, or when they were able to act in a way we don't often associate with Canadian MPs: free of partisan demands and eager to advance the interests of their constituents.

Was this anti-politician shtick the way MPs demonstrate solidarity with their constituents' distaste for political ambition? Taking an outsider stance allows MPs to distance themselves from the poor state of our politics, but this mindset can also offer a way to avoid taking responsibility and invariably diminishes the quality of politics for everyone.

"How would you describe the job of an MP?

"Well, I can give you the canned thing of why they tell us we're there, and I can share with you what I believe is the truth. So, in a nutshell, we're there to adopt national policy for the betterment of all in the country. The truth is: you're there to develop policy that is self-serving and beneficial to your party in order to keep you in power and get you re-elected. . . . There is politics involved in everything, so you kind of look at 'Okay, how many are we going to gain from this?' 'How does it fit with the principles of the party?' . . . That was the challenge of me deciding to become an MP: I've always been an independent thinker and the fact [is] that the majority of life was governed by someone else, and you had to adhere to the policy or [endure] the wrath of the whip." **Russ Powers**, *Liberal MP for Ancaster–*
Dundas–Flamborough–Westdale, 2004–06.

Is this what Powers set out to do when he ran for office? Exist in a system where the majority of his life "was governed by someone else"? Of course not. Nor did his fellow MPs aim to work in similar conditions. But change is not so easily accomplished.

In 1968, the American biologist Garrett Hardin published an essay in the journal *Science* called "The Tragedy of the Commons." In it, Hardin discusses the challenge of managing common resources. In his most famous example, Hardin describes the situation of a group of farmers who can freely graze their animals on a shared pasture. Facing no extra costs if they do so, each individual farmer has the incentive to add an extra cow or two to the herd. Over time, however, an excess of cows will nibble the pasture bare, rendering the commons useless to all involved. How to begin conserving the grass? Everyone has an incentive to conserve in the long run, but no one has the incentive, in the short term, to go first. In order to preserve the land, the farmers must all agree upon an appropriate way to share the commons. They might agree to divide the land among themselves, impose quotas on herd sizes or allocate blocks of grazing time. While no individual farmer wants to initiate working toward a solution, the group must agree to some remedy if they wish to preserve the utility of the commons over time.

Hardin neatly describes the age-old conundrum that occurs when individual short-term interests run up against the long-term interests of a group. In such cases, finding a solution demands that someone go first, despite the likelihood that they'll pay dearly for doing so. In Hardin's essay we saw an analogy to another tragedy in another Commons, facilitated, often unwittingly, by the very people elected to uphold and preserve it.

We hope the MPs' recollections both frustrate and inspire you, and above all that they revive in you a desire to identify what we all can do to improve Canada's democracy for those who are still to come.

CHAPTER ONE

The Best Intentions

In 1967 future Bloc Québécois MP Jean-Yves Roy was a CEGEP student in his home town of Rimouski when Quebec premier Daniel Johnson Sr. was visiting to open a new library. As Roy was coming out of the old library on a Saturday morning, bed-headed, he bumped into the premier and his entourage. Johnson struck up a conversation with Roy, who already happened to know quite a bit about politics at that point—enough, apparently, to impress the premier. Johnson invited the young man to the ribbon-cutting ceremony and later sent him a copy of his recently published book, *Égalité ou indépendance,* which Roy still has, along with Johnson's accompanying note, to this day. In 1969, the year after the premier's death, the next Union Nationale premier, Jean-Jacques Bertrand, introduced Bill 63, which was intended to promote the French language. But Roy didn't think it went far enough. He joined the Parti Québécois to fight against Bill 63. "I didn't have a career plan," Roy recalled. "I never did. I didn't have a specific career plan; I didn't tell myself when I was sixteen or seventeen that I would get into politics—I wasn't like that."

In his professional life, Roy became a teacher, then a journalist and editor. In 1981 came the first of a series of requests from the political world that had him spending the ensuing decades bouncing back and forth between public and private life. He was living in Pointe-au-Père, a small town near the mouth of the St. Lawrence River that has since been amalgamated with Rimouski, and the mayor invited him to become involved in municipal politics. He started out leading a recreation commission, became a municipal councillor and then ended up as mayor himself. Next, in 1984, Roy began working in Ottawa as a departmental assistant for Monique Vézina, a federal Progressive Conservative MP who'd recently been named to Cabinet as minister of supply and services by Prime Minister Brian Mulroney. He returned to Ottawa in 1993, this time to work as a departmental assistant for René Canuel, the Bloc MP who had recently been elected in the neighbouring riding of Matane–Matapédia.

One day, Roy visited a part of the riding that had no cell phone coverage. When he got home his wife gave him a message to call François Leblanc, Bloc leader Gilles Duceppe's chief of staff, as soon as possible.

"Your member resigned today after caucus," said Leblanc. "An election is going to be called on Sunday—and you have to run."

"Are you serious?" Roy replied. "There's no one else?"

"You have to run," Leblanc repeated, and gave him until six o'clock the next morning to think about it. Roy didn't want to run; the riding of Matane–Matapédia was enormous, encompassing the whole eastern half of the Gaspé Peninsula. Although Roy was well known in Rimouski, in other parts of the riding people didn't know him from Adam. He figured he wasn't likely to win; the Liberal candidate had a lot more name recognition than he did. So, he told us, "I called up all the people I thought might be interested in running, because I didn't want to run." None of them wanted to enter the race either. In fact, every one of them suggested that Roy would make the best candidate. After a sleepless night, he agreed, reluctantly, to stand as the nominee. The election took place on November 27, 2000, and Roy won by 276 votes. "My god," he exclaimed that night. "I have been elected! How can that be?" Even a man who'd served as mayor of a Quebec city and spent fourteen years working as an assistant for two different MPs on Parliament Hill, including a Cabinet minister, insisted: "I never in my entire life thought of going into politics."

Like Jean-Yves Roy, many of the eighty MPs we met went out of their way to suggest to us that they didn't *pursue* political office. From our first interviews, one salient feature about their initial forays into politics became evident. They had to be asked to run, and when they *were* asked, they said they'd been reluctant to accept. Some, like Roy, even claimed to have taken great pains to *avoid* running.

In time, we learned to take these avowals of reluctance with a grain of salt. In Roy's case, for example, we found it hard to fully credit that such a political insider, with his years of experience working on Parliament Hill, had never harboured at least a small inkling to serve as a Member of Parliament, or hadn't at least considered the notion at some point. Like many creation myths, this common narrative features elements that are difficult to take literally.

In politics, the narrative features a self-styled political outsider being asked by some party insider to pursue political office. At first the candidate is reluctant. Then external forces intervene—a convincing friend, or, as in Roy's case, an absence of other candidates. As the MP recounts it, he or she is *forced* to run. Holding his or her nose, no less! And then, against all probability, the reluctant candidate somehow ends up getting elected.

As origin stories go, the tale spun by our federal politicians is prototypically Canadian, with its disregard for ambition and its celebration of the underdog. Does it matter that we think these stories were somewhat contrived? We don't think so. Whether it's Adam and Eve and the serpent, or Zeus battling the titan Cronus, creation myths do tend to say something about the people who tell them. So what does the creation myth of the Canadian politician say about the people who lead this country?

THE FORMER MPS we interviewed frequently described their initial attitude toward politics as stronger than simple reluctance. Many portrayed themselves as having to be almost dragged, kicking and screaming, into the job. It was remarkable: before we learned anything else about them, these MPs wanted to make sure we grasped just how resistant they had been to entering politics. Furthermore, in discussing their lives before, during and after their political careers, they tended to portray themselves as having never fully embraced the job.

Take former MP for Fraser Valley West, Randy White. Before entering politics in the early '90s he was co-CEO and secretary-treasurer of his local school board in Abbotsford, a town in southern British Columbia. An accountant by profession, he was also the president of the Abbotsford Rotary Club. White was in the process of negotiating a new labour contract with striking teachers when the teachers' lead negotiator slid a book across the table toward him. "You sound like these guys," the negotiator said. It was the Reform Party's "Blue Book." "I *do* sound like these guys," thought White as he read it, He joined the party and became an organizer for his riding.

But who would be Reform's Fraser Valley West candidate in the next federal election? "We were all making six figures," White recalls. "[We] were lawyers, accountants and CEOs. Nobody really wanted to do it." He and his fellow Abbotsford Reformers developed a strategy: they would put forward a nominee and then attend the nomination meeting. Through their nominee, they'd try to exert some influence on the process—to make sure that their views were being discussed during the nomination race. At a meeting in a local law firm, White's friends talked him into running as the nominee the group would put forward. "You're the obvious choice," they said. "I don't know about this one," he replied.

White was already a busy man. "I had one hundred million dollars in capital going into building schools. We were the fastest-growing district in Canada." He went home and told his wife that his associates wanted him to run for the nomination, to try to become the Reform candidate. The idea was that a high-quality candidate like White would encourage other, similarly high-quality candidates to come forward to contest the Reform ticket.

"You're not getting elected, are you?" his wife asked. "Oh no," he tried to reassure her. But then his candidacy gained momentum. Few other viable candidates stepped forward, and donations were pouring in. "We've got cash galore here," White's associates said. "People are saying you're the right person for the job."

Even as the nomination meeting approached, White clung to the hope that someone else would beat him. "No, Randy's not going to win this," he told his associates. "Randy's going in to get the best person to win this. Remember, guys."

At the nomination meeting, White "blew out" about a half-dozen other contenders. He'd won the Reform ticket, and he grasped for the first time that he could win the election—he could become an MP. "Wait a minute," he said to himself. "I'm leaving my job if I win this? How much does an MP make anyway?" He wasn't thrilled to hear that, at the time, an MP only made $65,000. And when he told his wife it was looking as though he might win the race, news of the much smaller salary "went over like a lead balloon."

"Why are we going downhill like this?" his wife asked. But as the 1993 federal election approached, White realized the momentum was on his side. "We already knew we had it," he recalled. "We knew by the amount of money, and people, and votes." White ended up winning by 12,000 votes—almost, to hear him tell it, against his will.

ASK PEOPLE WHO WORK at demanding, stressful occupations— the emergency room doctors, high-school principals or Bay Street CEOs—and many will say they couldn't imagine doing anything else. Doing what they do was a goal. Whether the plan to get there was developed in high school, university or even later, these accomplished achievers had a plan: one they stuck to, one they scrimped and sacrificed to carry out, one that helped them rise to the important position that represented the pinnacle of their ambitions.

Not the MPs we interviewed.

"I was approached by someone heading up the search. They said, 'We are looking for someone to run for the nomination for Member of Parliament. We think we can win the seat,'" recalled Catherine Bell, a former cook. "I said, 'Oh, let me think, who could we get?' and he said, 'No, I mean you.' I hadn't really thought about it." She went on to win the 2006 election for the NDP in Vancouver Island North.

Jean Augustine, a high-profile community leader in the west end of Toronto who had immigrated to Canada from Grenada, was first approached to run by Toronto business executive and Conservative organizer John Tory. Augustine paraphrased his pitch: "Brian Mulroney is stepping down and Kim Campbell wants to go for it. . . . She is looking for some candidates and she is looking for women. He just thought I would be great." Augustine continued, "I said no, no, no, no, no. I don't see myself as running for politics." She saw herself providing input on policy, but not being the figure in the spotlight. She also declined the NDP when they approached her. And, finally, the Liberals came. "I had breakfast with them," she recalled. "Then I had lunch, then I had breakfast, then I had lunch, then I had dinner." And at some point during all that cultivating, Augustine figured, what did she have to lose? She went on to spend twelve years as an MP, from 1993 to 2005.

Ken Epp, a Reform-turned-Conservative MP from Alberta, had a similar story: "One of my friends, who was on the board of the constituency association and knew me personally, came to my door and said, 'We want you to run as our candidate.'" Epp laughed him off. "You've got to be kidding! That's not really in the cards." But the friend kept appearing at Epp's door, every three or four days, asking whether he would run as the Reform candidate. Finally, Epp became intrigued enough to arrange a meeting with Deborah Grey, the first-ever elected Reform MP, up in Edmonton. "If people of principle don't become involved in the political process," Grey told him, "then we are destined to be governed by those who have no principles." Finally, Epp gave in. He decided to pursue public office.

The point is, Epp *had* to give in. Politics wasn't a career he'd ever have considered on his own.

SO WHO WERE THESE apparently reluctant politicians? The MPs we interviewed arrived in federal politics typically in their mid-to-late forties, often having raised a family and built a career, usually far from Ottawa. Apart from the common "reluctant outsider" theme, their stories featured a remarkable diversity. Parliamentarians' backgrounds, family histories, cultures, levels of education and pre-political careers were far more varied and less predictable than we'd assumed. Some had been political party staffers but few were the consummate political insiders we had expected. They had not grown up in political dynasties; most had university degrees but they hadn't all studied political science or law, and few had long-standing political party involvement. "Politics wasn't something that anybody in my family actively participated in. . . . It just seemed what other people do," said John Cummins, the Conservative MP for Delta–Richmond East in B.C.

Before running for office, the MPs pursued a wide range of jobs, professions and community interests. More than a quarter were involved in education: as teachers, coaches, principals or academics. An even larger number were active in business, working as proprietors, managers, salespeople and senior executives. Others came from such professions as journalism, accounting, engineering, nursing, natural resources, farming and social work. Ten percent had some military experience, and many more worked in the public sector in a variety of roles—a civil-service manager, a police officer, an air traffic controller. Several ran non-profit organizations; others were involved in unions; two were clergymen. One was a grand chief. Their careers reflected the diversity of the country and the economy, although most enjoyed a middle-class lifestyle. Many had done a volunteer gig with a local political party association, maybe a stint as a municipal or provincial elected official or as an aide to a politician. They'd perhaps talked politics around the family table, but few had spent their young adulthoods waving a political party flag.

In our cohort of former MPs, there were nevertheless a few high-profile exceptions who had come from families that prioritized politics. We've already mentioned Liberal MP and former prime minister Paul Martin, who is the son of the Liberal MP and minister of finance. Former NDP leader Alexa McDonough's father, Lloyd Shaw, while never elected, was the first national research director of the NDP's precursor, the Co-operative Commonwealth Federation (CCF), and also the provincial secretary of the CCF's Nova Scotia wing. People like Tommy Douglas, a Saskatchewan premier, MP and first leader of the federal NDP, or M.J. Coldwell and Stanley

Knowles, both long-time MPs and senior statesmen in the party, were frequent visitors to the McDonough home. When they visited, they gathered around the family breakfast table or beside the fireplace debating any list of issues, local to international. McDonough knew life no other way. But what had inspired the rest to get into politics?

A few cited their upbringing—parents who talked politics at home or positions on student councils. Inky Mark, who represented the rural Manitoba riding surrounding Dauphin from 1997 until 2010, grew up on politics in an unconventional setting: waiting tables in his parents' Chinese restaurant in the 1950s and '60s. By the time he was nine, he was working attentively in the family business. "I grew up in the public," he said. "I heard lots of commentary about everything."

We've shared Bloc MP Jean-Yves Roy's story about his chance meeting with Premier Daniel Johnson Sr. Several other MPs cited pivotal points when their lives intersected with political leaders. The NDP's Bill Siksay recalled being a kid caught up in Trudeaumania in the 1960s. He and some school friends had gone to check out a rally in his hometown of Oshawa. Siksay ended up shaking Trudeau's hand at the rally and became hooked on politics. "I was a little groupie at that time and very excited about all of that," he said. "It was a very interesting and a very exciting time." Remarkably, his high school, R.S. McLaughlin, had an elaborate parliamentary system of student government. While most other schools had councils and presidents, McLaughlin had a House of Commons and a Senate. Each class sent its representative, their MP, to the House of Commons, and the Senate was appointed by the governor general, who was the principal. A staff advisor served as speaker. The student MPs ran in a wider election. If you won, you sat in Cabinet; if you lost, you were in opposition. Siksay was an MP for grade nine and eventually became the school prime minister.

WHEN CALLED TO SERVE in politics, our MPs told us, their reasons for ultimately saying yes were as varied as their lives and careers. Some felt drawn to politics out of a duty to serve a particular community. Take Loyola Hearn. In the late '90s, Hearn was working in Newfoundland for the provincial Progressive Conservatives. A teacher by profession, Hearn had served in the provincial legislature for the PCs from 1982 to 1993, including a stint as the minister of education from 1985 to 1989. But as the '90s were coming to a close, the PCs were in rough shape in Newfoundland. No money, no organization— and the polls suggested they'd be wiped out in the next election. Hearn helped assemble a team that encouraged a successful business executive, Danny Williams, to lead the party. Williams asked Hearn to stay on to help get the party back on a solid footing. "That threw me back into the active political scene," he said. "It wasn't that I was craving to get back [into public life] at all. It was more or less a duty, an obligation, a favour."

During that time, the Progressive Conservative MP in Hearn's riding resigned his seat, and the local guys urged Hearn to run. As prominent a political figure as Hearn was, even he was reluctant to pursue a position in Parliament. "They all said, 'Look. You're the ideal candidate. You're well known, and you have a good record. We are all here to help.'"

During those years, the Progressive Conservatives were also in rough shape at the federal level, still smarting from the lingering effects of the 1993 election, which had left them with only two seats. In 1998 former prime minister Joe Clark had come out of political retirement to hold things together, even though he didn't have a seat himself. In such a climate, Hearn figured a PC win in the riding would be tough. "I more or less said, 'Look. For the sake of the party, I'll run and put on a good campaign, but we'll have to work hard if we're going to win.' And we did."

Others saw pursuing public office as a way to learn and grow as professionals and as citizens. Sue Barnes had been a lawyer with her own law practice in London, Ontario, for fifteen years, and was ready for a change. "I needed a bigger challenge [and] was concerned if you got bored you could become negligent," she said. Barnes had considered the judiciary, but a mentor encouraged her toward politics. An element of obligation did creep into her decision, though. "[Being an immigrant], it was my payback to Canada," she said.

The majority of our interviewees, however, had taken a look at politics and found it wanting. They saw a system that didn't reflect them or what they viewed as important. Some believed the political system was moving in the wrong direction: that the link between government and citizens was broken, and prime ministers, red or blue, acted too frequently beyond accountability. In some cases, they'd grown to resent the leadership style of a particular prime minister and wished for something better. "I was pissed off," said Conservative MP Jay Hill. "I think that is probably what motivates quite a few people." And Chuck Strahl, first elected as a member of the Reform Party in 1993, reported: "There was a lot of anger in the West . . . especially toward the federal [Progressive]

Conservatives, . . . We felt let down. We felt that what we had tasked them to do in Ottawa, they had not done."

Others found a connection to politics in response to a particular local, regional or global event. Constitutional debates, the Charlottetown Accord and the Quebec referendums of 1980 and 1995 were lightning rods for several. Eleni Bakopanos, a Montreal-area Liberal MP, came of age during the first Quebec referendum. She sided firmly with Ottawa. "Definitely the 1980 referendum was the platform to launch my political career. . . . They can package it up any way they want to, but the fact is that [the separatists] want to divide the country. The country would not be the same, no matter how you slice it," she said. "I was very much motivated in terms of wanting to make a difference. I know it sounds so corny, but I did want to make a difference."

Some were more forthright contenders. "I am up for a challenge. I love when people wave a [matador's] big red cape in front of me because, of course, I want to charge at it," said Penny Priddy, a former NDP MP for Surrey North in British Columbia. And a few, like Colleen Beaumier, Liberal MP for Brampton from 1993 to 2008, admitted to both Bakopanos's purpose and Priddy's ambition: "I was a forty-six-year-old child who still thought she could save the world."

IN 2009, *The Economist* conducted an international survey of five thousand politicians by examining their entries in the *International Who's Who*. They noticed some idiosyncratic relationships between people in government and the countries they led. American political elites demonstrated a prevalence of lawyers; China tended to be ruled by engineers—at the time, its nine-member politburo comprised eight engineers, including President Hu Jintao, whose engineering specialty is hydraulics. Indonesia and much of Africa favour military men. Egypt (until recently) liked academics. In South Korea, it's civil servants, and in Brazil, it's doctors. "Different countries—because of their history, or cultural preferences, or stage of development—seem to like particular qualities, and these qualities are provided disproportionately by only a few professions," *The Economist* opined.

Canada didn't feature in *The Economist*'s report. But in our research, we found no such correlation between MPs and their previous occupations. That diversity is encouraging: it suggests we don't have an established and difficult-to-penetrate "political class." You don't need to have attended certain schools or be a millionaire. There is no direct path to entering politics in this country, no clearly identified and understood "farm team." In other countries the profession of politics may be reserved for those with economic or social means, but in Canada the political field is relatively accessible, and open as well to people born outside the country. Although most MPs have some form of post-secondary education and more credentials than the average Canadian, their pre-political occupational diversity reflects the diversity of Canadians' employment more closely than we likely realize.

Few examples make this point as well as that of former NDP MP Catherine Bell of Vancouver Island North, who worked in a kitchen before rising up through the union ranks into contention for a seat in Parliament. She knew things were heating up during her 2006 campaign when a reporter from the *National Post* called her one day and asked, "What is a cook going to bring to Ottawa? And how do you think you're qualified for this position?" Her response? "Well, maybe that's what we need is some more diversity. . . . It's called the House of Commons for a reason. It's for Canadians of all walks of life, having a say and their views represented. I don't think that only lawyers and accountants have the ability to do that."

No matter what our MPs' varied backgrounds, their transitions from ordinary citizen to political leader were marked by what they described as a series of random occurrences. A political career was something they claimed not to have planned for or worked toward. Few admitted to ever considering politics as a career goal, let alone aspiring to work as an MP, a member of Cabinet or prime minister. Nearly all said they had been asked to run, usually by an acquaintance involved in a political party or someone from a community group. Many claimed they had not expected to be asked, and that they had responded initially with reluctance. While some reluctance is understandable—politics is far from a secure business, and there are usually family or career considerations—the persistence of this narrative among so many divergent candidates was surprising. Even those who acknowledged that they'd considered making a run for office at some point in their lives still claimed to be surprised when that moment arrived.

Former Liberal MP Anne McLellan, who represented her Edmonton riding from 1993 until 2006, is one example. She grew up on a dairy farm in Nova Scotia. Her parents were political: her dad was in the Liberal party; her mom was a municipal councillor who would eventually become the county's deputy reeve. McLellan herself was involved with the Liberal

Party as a student at Dalhousie University in Halifax. She remained involved as a law professor at the University of New Brunswick, and later, as a professor at the University of Alberta's law school, at least in part because it offered her ways of meeting people in a province where she was a newcomer.

"I really just wasn't thinking about running," she said. Then in the summer of 1992 a critical care nurse named Claire Laskin, whom McLellan had met at various Liberal functions, came up and broached the topic of McLellan running as a candidate. "I've heard you speak a number of times," Laskin said. "There is a group of us who would work with you. We'll work to get the nomination. We know that a Liberal hasn't been elected in Alberta in twenty-five years."

McLellan was reluctant, and said so. Laskin asked her to take the summer vacation to think about it. In the course of the summer, McLellan decided to give it a whirl. But she under-scores that the possibility wouldn't have occurred to her, had Laskin not approached her out of the blue. "I would not have run for political office if this woman had not shown up at my door and said, 'Anne, we'd like you to try and do this.'"

A SURVEY OF 170 Liberal and 168 NDP candidates from the 2008 election, initiated by political scientists William Cross and Lisa Young, asked a number of questions about what had motivated those candidates, both successful and otherwise, to run for office. Of the 186 respondents, 66 percent indicated that encouragement by family, friends and support from others in community groups to which the candidate belonged were important factors. This finding supports the picture of our typical Member of Parliament so far. But Cross and Young made another finding that leads us to another compelling force in these MPs' decision to seek office. For 75 percent of these respondents, party recruitment—usually involving the local riding association, although sometimes involving only the party's national leadership—had also played a role in their decision.

Candidates recruited by local party associations were much more likely to have been involved in the community in which they lived. According to Cross and Young's study, 76 percent of locally recruited candidates were involved in more than five civil society organizations, while only 44 percent of those recruited by the national party, and 21 percent of those who self-nominated, claimed the same. Locally chosen candidates were also more likely than others to have given significant volunteer time to the associations to which they belonged. They were more often female and much more likely to be members of ethnic associations than those who put themselves forward as candidates. As it turns out, they were also much more likely to win.

So, when we heard many MPs describe themselves as political outsiders, it struck us as strange. Their self-description seemed at odds with the extent of their involvement in their own communities. Notwithstanding their wide variety of backgrounds and perspectives, many future parliamentarians had worked or volunteered in some capacity in the proverbial "public square," as journalists, teachers or social workers. Others had served as provincial politicians, or supplemented their day jobs with positions on a school board or municipal council. Many volunteered in community associations, some in unions. So, whether through their profession, their volunteer commitments, or a combination of both, they had the opportunity to interact with a cross-section of their community.

Through this work in the public sphere, they had discovered they had the power to successfully create change, however minuscule or substantial its form, even if they didn't see that community work as necessarily "political." They either liked the taste of their accomplishments, or they saw a great potential for change. One MP recalled serving as the president of the local Chamber of Commerce when his town's major employer announced widespread cuts. "It was a really difficult time for the community," said former Liberal MP Andy Mitchell, who served in the riding of Parry Sound–Muskoka from 1993 to 2006. "You had young men who were mostly hard-rock miners in their twenties and thirties [whose well-paying jobs] just disappeared overnight." The future MP became heavily involved with the community's response and realized that the work he was doing with his fellow citizens could lead to positive change. It was also a lesson in how government mattered. "The policy the provincial and federal governments were going to pursue in response was going to make a difference in individual people's lives. That rekindled an earlier interest and my involvement in politics has been pretty consistent since then."

Others, seeing a system that excluded people, a community that was struggling or an institution that was out of touch, were motivated to do something about it. Carol Skelton, a Conservative MP from Saskatchewan, had a job that involved visiting women in rural communities. This work provided a unique insight into poverty on the prairies. "I don't know how many women I saw there that were trying to get enough money just to survive," Skelton said. "The social infrastructure in agricultural communities at that time was a problem."

Former Liberal MP Claudette Bradshaw had worked with abused children in her home province of New Brunswick. She was spurred toward politics by the news that one of her now-grown-up "kids" had murdered someone. "The child was really abused. We tried to get him out of the area he was in," she recalled. "Government wouldn't listen and we couldn't get anything done for this child. When he went into the school system he became very aggressive. His mother, when he was six, said, 'Is he going to have to kill somebody to get help?' Well, at the age of twenty-one he did. So [my spouse said], 'You have to go to Ottawa. Somebody's got to go. They've got to understand.'"

In other words, those who were asked to run for office were very much a part of the communities in which they lived. "In the end, I guess it was the community members that came to me when there was going to be an opening to run . . . they saw me as a person who had been engaged in public life in the sense of being an advocate in our local community," said Paul Macklin, the Liberal MP for the Ontario riding of Northumberland–Quinte West from 2000 to 2006.

A few MPs—and they were the exceptions—said they actively pursued their candidacy. Take John Godfrey, a former academic then editor of the *Financial Post*, who'd always thought he'd like to give politics a shot. "It was on the bucket list," he said. By 1993 Godfrey was so enthusiastic about pursuing public office that he ignored the Liberal Party's wishes and jumped ridings from Markham, north-east of Toronto, where he'd been working to build some presence, to

Don Valley West, a riding closer to downtown, where he would go on to win six consecutive elections.

Why is it that so few of our federal politicians claimed to want to be federal politicians? One might say it's simply an aspect of our unpredictable world; few of us work at the jobs we had imagined when we were young. But would we be embarrassed by the jobs we do? We were startled that, even after the fact, our MPs consistently were so reluctant to identify themselves as politicians. They explained away any political ambition, or were apologetic about it.

The evidence of our MP interviews, together with the research of Cross and Young, suggests that actively pursuing public office, or at least admitting to actively pursuing public office, is rare in Canadian political culture. Cross and Young's study indicates that those who intentionally pursue a political career, at least in the two parties they surveyed, suffer at the ballot box. Those who self-nominate, who also tended to be male and to have revealed careerist or policy-related motives for running, are much less likely to become MPs.

Do our system and our national sensibilities resist those who self-select for public office? Do Canadians prefer a form of community endorsement and a candidacy unsullied by ambition? Or does the reluctance to admit to political ambition speak of something more pernicious: that a belief that politics, unlike most other demanding professions, is something for which one cannot admit ambition? No doubt it's a reflection of the bad odour in which candidates realize Canadians hold their elected leaders. Canadian society seems not only to frown on political ambition—it frowns on politicians themselves. Statistics and surveys bear this out. EKOS Research data show that the proportion of Canadians who trust their government to do the right thing has decreased from nearly 60 percent in 1968 to 28 percent in 2012. "The mistrust in government is much more focused on politicians and political parties, not officials," wrote EKOS president Frank Graves. "The paucity of trust in politicians is almost cartoonishly low." A different EKOS survey rated Canadian trust in various professions. Nurses and doctors rated high, with about 80 percent professing a high level of trust for these well-known clinical professions. Politicians were at the bottom of the pack, with only 10 percent professing a high degree of trust. The only profession that ranked below politicians? Internet bloggers. A similar poll, the 2013 Trust Poll of 2,020 people conducted by Leger Marketing for Reader's Digest Canada, ranked politicians as the second-least trusted profession. Who ranked lower in this survey? Psychics.

Our politicians' attitudes reflect the data. In other words, even our politicians have a negative view of their own kind—such a negative view, apparently, that they are reluctant to admit interest or ambition in their own line of work. So perhaps our ballot boxes suggest that Canadians like a little reluctance—genuine or otherwise—in the people we choose as our leaders.

TIME AND TIME AGAIN, we encountered MPs taking pains to portray themselves as outsiders looking to fix a flawed political system. Few used the exact word "outsider," but certainly many made a point of underscoring how different they were from regular politicians. In other words, they were eager to secure their credibility as ordinary, concerned Canadians.

"It couldn't have happened to a guy who fit the role less. Since when is the busboy supposed to become an MP?" asked Liberal Don Boudria, whose first job in Parliament was clearing tables in the parliamentary dining room, and who styled his political career as an *Upstairs, Downstairs* story. "Somehow, with lots of luck and some elbow grease, it worked out. But still, it leaves a few people scratching their heads."

In some instances, this outsiderism was geographical (and, arguably, realistic). The size and regional nature of Canada alone can give citizens a sense of feeling a world apart from the capital. MPs from distant communities wanted to put their constituency on the map. "I wanted Ottawa to know where Vancouver Island North was," said Catherine Bell. "It was about as far away from Ottawa as you can get."

For others, the outsider stance was rooted in ideology or the need for policy change. Ideologically oriented MPs articulated how their outlook on life, political philosophy or perspective on a policy issue wasn't adequately acknowledged in the system. "I'm an accountant by profession, and was acutely aware of what the damage was to our next generation of our deficits accumulating at $40 billion per year," said Randy White. Anne McLellan, describing what initially made her accept the invitation to run, cited her own strong "views on the future of the country, national unity and the role of the government in Canada."

And sometimes it was a matter of personal identity. Most women were aware that, despite advances in some fields, politics remains a male-dominated profession. "I had no role models. There was no black woman who was in the Parliament of Canada, and no black woman was at Queen's

Park or any other place I could look at," said Jean Augustine. One aboriginal MP was conscious of past exclusion. "My mom, she's seventy-five and she remembers when she wasn't allowed to leave the reserve. She needed a pass. So you are battling that history," said Gary Merasty, the former Liberal MP for Saskatchewan's Desnethé–Missinippi–Churchill River riding.

For immigrants, moving to a new country is often such an integral part of their experience that it plays into the dynamics of their self-identification. "The majority can't [appreciate] the struggle that a minority feels," said Saudi Arabian–born Omar Alghabra, a Liberal MP from Mississauga–Erindale. And Marlene Catterall, the daughter of a German immigrant, recalls approaching Parliament right after her election as a Liberal MP from Ottawa, still thinking of her family as relative newcomers: "I remember walking up the steps to go into the Centre Block and thinking, 'Okay, Daddy, so what's the daughter of a lousy immigrant tailor doing here?' My dad had just died about six months before and you know, he would have loved to see this."

And even some new MPs with prior, more local, political experience expressed a sense of feeling out of place in the wider political arena. "I've always been driven by trying to represent the people who elect me. That's what motivated me: to represent them as best I could in Ottawa and be the voice for the small guy. I always put my riding and my province first, sometimes to my own peril," said Bill Matthews, a Newfoundland MP from 1997 until 2004, who had earlier served fourteen years as a provincial politician.

THE TWO NARRATIVE components of our interviews—reluctance to pursue a political career, and the maverick "anti-political" sensibility once in office—seem to be caused by, and perpetuate, the same negative perception of politics and the people who work inside the system. The cynical public does not believe it, and it discourages high-calibre candidates from pursuing public office. "Once politicians start pretending they're not politicians, but their opponents are, it has the effect, not just of driving voters away from their opponents, but of driving them away from the political system itself," said former Liberal leader Michael Ignatieff in a 2012 speech at Stanford University on partisanship. "If politicians don't start sticking up for their own profession voters certainly won't."

Would the calibre of our politicians improve, and would politicians become perceived as more trustworthy, if our elected representatives chose *other* narratives about themselves? Andrew Potter's 2010 book, *The Authenticity Hoax*, observes that contemporary politicians and the parties that back them are marketed just like consumer goods, a phenomenon he refers to as "the Big Macification of civil discourse." The trouble, however, is in the tactics that Canadian politicians often employ to market their brands. The advertising world features many cases where two or more brands compete for a limited market share—a situation analagous to the competition for electoral votes. But we don't see advertisements from Coca-Cola or Pepsi criticizing the soft-drink industry. Nor do we see McDonald's and Burger King criticizing fast food. "Why doesn't Kenneth Cole go after Ralph Lauren?" Potter asks in his book. "Because it would run the risk of turning the public off the entire category and shrinking sales for all concerned."

Unfortunately, Canadian politics, with its outsider-identifying, maverick candidates, has not yet shared this insight.

Our common cultural history seems to include a period when politics was perceived as an esteemed calling, a respected profession, a time when fine and upstanding men and women enthusiastically pursued the honour of party candidacy and political office. Our interviews with former Canadian MPs reflect that those romantic notions are long gone, if they ever actually existed. (The exact moment when the tide turned is open to discussion.) Today, politics is considered such an unsavoury pursuit, the MPs tell us, that people must be harangued, corralled—sometimes conscripted—into pursuing public office. Even if being elected is a private dream, the most palatable way to market one's candidacy involves at least a tacit separation from, and criticism of, politics, perpetuating the negative stereotypes. With outlooks like that, it would seem that we're lucky anyone chooses to run at all.

CHAPTER TWO

Out of the Frying Pan . . .

A fter the decision to run for federal politics, the next waypoint toward a seat as a Member of Parliament is the nomination—the contest every political party is meant to hold when numerous citizens compete to become its official candidate in a particular riding. If ever a political party mandated clean nomination contests for itself, it was the Reform Party. Founded by Preston Manning and supporters in 1987, Reform was established on the principle of participatory democracy, the belief that citizens should have a greater say in the way their governments run their country. "If we wanted the operations of the federal government and Canadian constitutional relationships to reflect such principles, we had to be consistent in applying them to ourselves," Manning wrote in a memoir. "We were to be an open, transparent organization in which every member was treated equally and fairly."

Hence the focus on clean nomination battles. One of the Reform Party's early classics happened in the riding of Medicine Hat, Alberta, on April 11, 1992. Candidate Monte Solberg can remember stepping off the bus and into the city's Cypress Centre that evening and being astonished at the number of people at the convention. Maybe 10,000, all told. Medicine Hat, with a population of about 60,000, is the largest city in southeastern Alberta, and Solberg's seven fellow nominees included some of the city's best-known citizens. The president of the Medicine Hat Chamber of Commerce was going for the nomination, as well as the owner of the local VW dealership. The night's favourite was Kathy Mandeville, a Medicine Hat alderman.

If he was a long shot, Solberg had hustle on his side. None of his competitors, he felt, had such a hardworking group of supporters. Solberg was the manager of the local radio station in Brooks, a town of about 10,000 people located an hour away from Medicine Hat. Solberg's camp realized the nomination venue of Medicine Hat put them at a disadvantage. A big fish in Medicine Hat would attract more support than a big fish from the small pond of Brooks. So Solberg's camp did their best to bring Brooks to Medicine Hat: they chartered school buses and packed them full of supporters—150 in all.

In his nomination speech, Solberg did his best to reflect the concerns of the people who'd attended the town hall meetings he'd held in the lead-up to the nomination. "The most important aspect of it was, we want you to represent our views to Ottawa, not the other way around," Solberg recalled later. "People had just had it. They were really frustrated. So I did my best to channel that . . . My goal was to make sure *they* understood *I* understood what they were saying, and to convince them I would listen to them."

Sometime around ten o'clock, the returning officer, Elwin Hermanson, took the microphone to give the results. Solberg 403 votes, Mandeville 400, and a local business executive, David Humphries, a distant third with 97. Solberg was in the lead, but without the majority required to win. There'd have to be another vote.

Before that happened, one candidate withdrew, then another, leaving the three leaders and three other candidates on the ballot for the second round. Balloons waved. Supporters thrust placards skyward. Outbursts of enthusiasm broke out spontaneously and then faded, and then erupted again elsewhere in the convention centre. Within the hour, Hermanson took the stage a second time to announce the results. Solberg and Mandeville were tied at 456 votes apiece.

Third ballot, two candidates. Now Solberg could see that people were leaving. The rumour went around that they were the distant folks, the folks who had long car rides out of town—or to Brooks. Were Solberg's supporters going home? By the time the third round of voting started, Solberg was exhausted. The ballots disappeared to be counted by Hermanson and his crew, and the place waited. So much was at stake. Solberg thought about his friends, and how much work everyone had put into getting him the nomination. He wanted to win for their sake.

For the third time, Hermanson came out to announce the results. By this time it was almost midnight. Hermanson leaned into the microphone. What did he say, exactly? Solberg couldn't remember. He remembered only the results— Mandeville 485, Solberg 487.

Solberg 487. Pandemonium! People pushed Solberg onstage amid a thousand handshakes. "It was utter relief, and joy at the same time," Solberg said. He gave a mostly incoherent acceptance speech. He was stunned. To win by two votes! He congratulated the other candidates—he could remember doing that.

The buses had made the difference. Yes, some delegates had left before the third ballot, but those turned out to be the Medicine Hat people, people who had their own cars, who could drive home at will. Solberg hadn't planned it this way, but the Brooks contingent was trapped in the Cypress Centre Auditorium that evening because the buses they'd arrived on weren't leaving until the ballots yielded a winner.

Solberg went on to take Medicine Hat in the upcoming federal election with 54 percent of the votes, a margin of 14,000. He would run again, and again, winning five consecutive federal elections; in his last run for office, he took 80 percent of the vote. He spent fifteen years as an MP, and three of those as a Cabinet minister for Stephen Harper, before retiring from politics in 2008. And in the years after his victory, when he was in his riding, strangers would come up to him and say: "I was at that nomination meeting. I was there, and I voted for you. It was *my* vote that helped put you over."

They remembered the exciting night in 1992 when Monte Solberg became the Reform Party candidate for Medicine Hat, Alberta. "People would tell me it was the most exciting thing they'd ever been a part of," Solberg would say later. "It really was a chance to participate in democracy. Those opportunities don't come along very often. In a lot of parties, nominations are protected, and it's hard to unseat the incumbent, and there's lots of things that work against real democracy breaking out. It was all about the excitement of being able to choose a new candidate—and to be a part of the democratic process."

OPEN AND TRANSPARENT nominations really can engage people in the democratic process, as the story of Solberg's nomination shows. In fact, they exemplify the way many Canadians believe nomination battles work—ideally, an open call for candidates, who then compete for support among the riding's party members in an election that is overseen by a leadership that takes pains to minimize any bias or perception of favouritism. Idealistic politicos envision the process as being coordinated by the local riding association, which is both the local representation of a political party and the organization charged with identifying, selecting and supporting candidates.

Unfortunately, few nominations take place as Monte Solberg's did. Time and again during the exit interviews we conducted, without prompting, MPs complained about the nomination processes. We'd initially asked how they got into politics merely to break the ice, and to give them an opportunity to talk about their early lives. Nevertheless, the MPs spent a great deal of time describing how painful and mystifying they found this particular aspect of their entry into politics. They said the nomination process was wild and unpredictable. Nasty. Unclean, and sometimes corrupt. They also said it was opaque— it was difficult for them to discern the rules, and how an ideal nomination process should go. The impression formed from the MPs' accounts? A political party often regards the nomination process as an inconvenient detour on the way to installing its preferred candidate as the party nominee, rather than as an important process that gives the party's riding supporters a mechanism to select the candidate they favour. It's here, in the nomination process, that our MPs first encountered the bullying and controlling behaviour of their parties.

"There's too much power in the hands of the central campaign committee," said former Oakville-area Liberal MP

Bonnie Brown. "They don't recognize the need for the local associations to have their own way. In other words, what they do is, they try to interfere and get the person they think can get elected nominated. . . . Then they wonder why all the other Liberals in town aren't working very hard. Instead of having a proper process and letting the best person in the eyes of the local Liberals win, and then everybody gets on board and you have a great team."

Such criticisms of the nomination process are of concern because political nomination is the point of entry into politics, the crucial first step in our electoral process. That moment is a key moment of engagement for regular citizens, and often their first contact with the political system. A nomination may give a first impression of what politics is like from the inside— and the way this first impression goes can either encourage or discourage people from further participation. Judging from Monte Solberg's encounters with former supporters, his first nomination turned a lot of people on to politics. To what extent are "opaque" and apparently predetermined nomination proceedings turning people off?

Although some MPs leave their parties once in office, in the past thirty years only two have been elected independently of a party. So, nominations also form many candidates' first impressions of working with a political party.

Working with an established party to win a seat in the House of Commons is supposed to be a three-step process: first, the party's riding association organizes a nomination contest to determine which party member will be its candidate for that riding. Next, the nominee's candidacy must be approved by the party leader. Then comes the election itself.

The nomination process is particularly important in Canada because many federal ridings tend to be won by the same political party, election after election. In recent decades, Toronto and Vancouver have largely voted Liberal, Winnipeg NDP and Alberta Conservative. Newfoundland tends to be Conservative in rural areas and Liberal in St. John's. The Quebec riding of Mount Royal has been Liberal since 1940. Ottawa–Vanier and its predecessor riding of Ottawa East have been Liberal since 1935. And Central Nova has been Conservative or Progressive Conservative for thirty of the last forty years. Of course, ridings do change hands, often as part of a wave—such as the 1993 election that nearly obliterated the Progressive Conservative Party, and the 2011 election, in which the Bloc Québécois lost forty-four of its forty-seven seats—but the preponderance of safe ridings in this country means that the nomination contest is effectively the real election.

At first glance, the nomination procedure seems straightforward: the delegate with the most votes wins the nomination. But even years after their first nomination, many of the MPs we interviewed struggled to articulate how nominations functioned, citing a lack of clarity in time lines, sources of decision making and the application of the rules. Procedures varied widely from riding to riding, and the process appeared subject to a host of idiosyncrasies, giving the impression that the party's, rather than the people's, favoured candidate was selected.

The power that parties exert over the nomination processes increased in two ways during the early '70s, as the result of a law passed in Parliament in 1970. Up until the 1972 federal election, ballots listed the names of candidates, along with their occupations—which provided a small personal touch. Although candidates had been affiliated with parties since Confederation, it wasn't until that election that the candidate's name was followed by an identifying political party. According to research prepared by the Parliament of Canada, the intention was to make it easier for voters to differentiate the candidates (there had been cases of candidates with similar names running in the same riding); and listing party affiliation seemed more in step with practices of modern political campaigning, in which parties and their leaders are often front and centre.

It's easy to read volumes of symbolic meaning in the change. Previously, candidates were individuals whose identity was informed by their job and perhaps the riding in which they lived. Once the candidate's name was followed by his or her party affiliation, the candidate became an extension of the party's brand. A second change further increased the candidate's subordination to the party, as party leaders gained veto power over each successful nominee. Before this change, local constituency associations would organize and oversee nomination races. But the new legislation empowered the party leader to refuse to sign someone's nomination papers, even if he or she had won the local nomination organized by the constituency association. From this point on, each candidate's accountability was fractured. Whereas candidates had once been accountable only to their local party association, they would also now serve the party leader—and the party leader began exercising that power.

According to research published in 2011 by political scientists Royce Koop and Amanda Bittner, these changes were embraced most enthusiastically by the Liberal Party, which amended its party constitution in the 1990s to give the party leader the ability to parachute in candidates, or pre-empt local nomination contests and appoint candidates with little or no input from members of a local riding association. In practice, however, this power is used sparingly. Its ostensible purpose is to increase the representation of women or other underrepresented groups, to appoint "star" candidates and to protect incumbents from well-organized local challengers. Yet in 2008, according to Koop and Bittner's research, roughly one in five members of the Liberal caucus had been helped through the nomination by the leader.

It wasn't only Liberals who had problems with the way the parties run nominations. The former Conservative MP for Saskatoon–Rosetown–Biggar, Carol Skelton, disapproved of the machinations of what she called the "backroom boys." Skelton said, "It was one of those things I didn't like about politics." Her colleague, former Conservative MP for Kelowna Werner Schmidt, called the process "scary" and "frightening." Inky Mark, a Manitoba MP for thirteen years, was scathing. "Parties are basically dishonest; totally dishonest. They lie through their teeth and manipulate their membership," he said. "They take all they want. It's a money grab. They grab your money. All the stuff they tell you to do is just a façade. It's like a TV commercial."

The former NDP MP for Winnipeg North, Judy Wasylycia-Leis, called her nomination process a really "eye-opening" situation. "I think, even though you might find that the NDP is more participatory and democratic than the Conservatives and the Liberals, I think . . . when we are in government, or close to being in government, we run into much more controlling situations that might be seen as the antithesis of true democracy." Principally, Wasylycia-Leis mentioned candidate recruitment.

"You have all this great theory on paper about searching for candidates, and 'we are never going to do what the Liberals do in terms of appointing candidates' and 'we are never going to do what the Conservatives do' . . . but I think sometimes what we do is, we control the timing and . . . we can find ways to make it impossible for anyone to contest a nomination. I think there is some real angst in the party right now about that."

Liberal Stephen Owen recounted his transition from law professor at the University of Victoria to Liberal candidate for Vancouver Quadra in the space of a week, after MP Ted McWhinney retired suddenly a week before Jean Chrétien's government called the 2000 election. "There was no time for a nomination meeting because the election would have been almost over by the time someone had been nominated, so I was going to have to be appointed by the prime minister, which is never a particularly popular thing," Owen said. "We were in an election within a week. Five weeks later we were standing before Parliament Hill."

Owen's case was exceptional—there wasn't time for a standard nomination process. Another exception belonged to Liberal MP Pierre Pettigrew, whom Jean Chrétien appointed to his Cabinet before Pettigrew had a seat in the House of Commons, an emergency measure to bolster federalist experience following the close result in the 1995 Quebec sovereignty referendum. It wasn't until MP André Ouellet was named the head of Canada Post, opening up the Montreal riding of Papineau–Saint-Michel, that Pettigrew was parachuted into the riding as the Liberal nominee and won the by-election on March 25, 1996.

The Liberals gave Eleni Bakopanos her riding of Saint-Denis in 1993 after Jean Chrétien insisted, against Bakopanos's wishes, that she not run in a conventional nomination race—part of a push by Chrétien and his team to elect more women into the House of Commons. And Jean Augustine, former MP for Etobicoke–Lakeshore, had experienced a similar selection process the same year. "That appointment marred a lot of debates and discussions that I was involved in. Whether it was the media, community, all-candidates' [debates], the whole business of 'you were appointed' came in," she recalled. Controversial nomination proceedings continued through the mid-2000s, as the Liberal Party transitioned from Chrétien's leadership to Paul Martin's guard. One well-known case involves the 2004 nomination battle in a newly formed Hamilton-area riding that encompassed ridings held by two sitting Liberal MPs. The ensuing contest cost former deputy PM Sheila Copps her seat. Another case was the 2004 Ottawa South race between David McGuinty and Ottawa city councillor Diane Deans, who claimed that senior party members asked her to step aside so that McGuinty would be certain to win the nomination. She declined, then lost the nomination contest anyway.

Or take the nomination battle of Omar Alghabra, an engineer and long-time Liberal Party member who worked on many different campaigns over the years. He was on the board of directors for the riding of Mississauga–Erindale, where a spot opened up after Liberal leader Paul Martin expelled the riding's MP, Carolyn Parrish, from caucus in 2004 following controversial comments about George W. Bush and her publicly stated antipathy toward Martin himself.

"Some people said, you should consider doing this, and then I actually shrugged it off," Alghabra recalls. "My immediate reaction was, no, are you kidding? I had my corporate blinders on. I had a career, I had a good job. . . . All the negative associations with being a professional politician came to mind, whether it is how people label politicians or the gruelling tasks of fundraising, campaigning." Then Alghabra had a conversation with a friend whom Alghabra had always badgered about getting involved in politics as a volunteer. Otherwise, Alghabra would say, just a handful of insiders had power. Now the friend told Alghabra that this was *his* chance—here was Alghabra's opportunity to get inside the process. To put his money where his mouth was.

Alghabra decided to go for it. He filled out the paperwork required to begin his candidacy in October of 2005, weeks before the Liberal minority government fell—a complex and detailed form that also included police and credit checks. And then he waited. There was a long conversation with Charles Bird, the Liberal Party's Ontario campaign manager. The telephone call felt like a job interview, Alghabra thought. Bird followed Alghabra's answers with impenetrable silence. Alghabra can recall thinking, once he ended the call, that he'd messed up somehow. In typically opaque fashion, the party didn't tell him anything about his application.

As time passed, Alghabra heard whispers about the Liberal Party's nomination proceedings. Was Martha Hall Findlay going to be parachuted into his riding, as an appointed Liberal Party nominee? What about Bob Rae? Altogether, Alghabra figures he'd heard that ten other people were interested in the nomination. "Like everything in politics," Alghabra says, "there were a lot of rumours and innuendo about what the party was going to do."

On the evening of Sunday, November 27, 2005, Alghabra picked up the phone to hear Charles Bird's voice. In a business-like manner, Bird informed him that the nomination meeting would happen in four days, on Thursday, December 1, at Mississauga's Canadian Coptic Centre. Alghabra would be running against Charles Sousa—a friend of Alghabra's, whom Alghabra had actually supported in earlier nomination battles.

What happened to the others who were supposedly interested in the riding? Did Liberal Party leadership interfere in the process, to increase the chances that the riding's party membership would elect someone—Alghabra or Sousa—whom the party found acceptable? Why did Bird interview Alghabra as he did? Shouldn't any Liberal Party member have been able to run in the riding, regardless of Bird's opinion? Alghabra didn't have time to pay much attention to those questions when he was just four days away from the biggest opportunity in his political life. He would eventually win the nomination, by 203 votes over Sousa, then go on to win Mississauga–Erindale in the 39th federal election by a count of more than three thousand, with 44.8 percent of the popular vote.

Alghabra had found the process uncomfortable, and wondered if there might not be a bigger role for a neutral body, such as Elections Canada, to better oversee the process—a belief several other MPs shared.

ANOTHER BONE OF contention expressed by many of the former MPs was the way party memberships were sold to win nominations. It is common practice that if a candidate isn't certain of support from the riding's current party membership, he or she may opt to bring in new people, more likely to be supporters, by selling them new party memberships. It's also a great way to get new people involved in the process, with the idea that they'll stick with you and lend a hand when the general election rolls around.

For example, to win the Liberal candidacy in the riding of Simcoe North in 1993, Paul DeVillers had to beat Alan Gray Martin, a former Liberal MP who had served one term in the 1970s and had run as the riding's Liberal candidate in the previous three elections, losing each time. DeVillers and others in the riding were certain Martin would lose a fourth time. "That's when I decided I'd take a shot at it," DeVillers said. He spent the next twenty-one days selling memberships—twelve hundred in all. He ended up beating Martin on the first ballot, and would go on to serve twelve years as an MP.

Such strategies can limit political office to those with time and energy to persuade people to sign up, or to those with financial means; for example, many candidates need to take time off to run.

When asked to comment on the nomination process, one MP volunteered that the process can cost a lot of money— for a different reason. "Personally?" we asked. "Oh, absolutely," the MP replied. "Who do you think pays for these memberships? Please, give me a break. You know politicians, when they get caught [buying memberships], say, 'Oh, I didn't know.' Well if they didn't know then they're bloody stupid. And this will continue to happen all the time with this system."

Our MPs drew attention to discrepancies between federal election rules and party nomination rules. In federal elections, voters must be eighteen years of age, but in some nomination races, younger teenagers had memberships and cast ballots. The younger demographic may have played a role in the nomination win of former high school principal Charles Hubbard, the Liberal MP for Miramichi from 1993 to 2008. His nomination meeting attracted four thousand people and lasted ten or eleven hours. He won on the fourth ballot. "We had thousands of so-called Liberal members," Hubbard said. "In fact, for this constituency, it was in excess of twenty thousand people who could have come. Memberships were free and just about everybody over fourteen years of age was signed up."

MPs also wondered about how nomination battles were affected by exploitation of identity and category politics, including the power wielded by religious institutions, ethnic groups and single-issue lobbies. Several felt that citizens were subject to manipulation by figures of influence within the party association. In some cases there were stories of groups of people being bussed in from other ridings on the day of the convention, solely to vote for a specific candidate. Citizens were often simply corralled for the event and asked only to sign up for a party membership, show up and vote for their candidate. They were not asked to contribute to the party's discussions in any meaningful way. "The part I found troubling was creating instant supporters," said Pat O'Brien, a former Liberal and independent MP for the riding of London–Fanshawe. "There were people who would come for one night to a party function, support the candidate of their choice, and not come again."

This, together with the way ethnic communities are engaged in politics in some parts of the country, left MPs feeling very uncomfortable. Bonnie Brown, the Oakville-area Liberal MP, described how it worked. "It's easier to raise money if you have an ethnic group," she said. "You're in a competition . . . and that Greek guy . . . when it comes time to raise money or to sell memberships, he goes around to all the Greek restaurants and Greek businesses and he gives—he just hands the owner say twenty-five membership forms," she said. He doesn't need to give any instruction—the business owners just know they want their guy in Parliament to represent their views, she said.

Brown described how candidates used fundraisers to curry favour with party leaders. She described one young man, an aspiring MP whose father raised the money his son needed and sent it to the party leader. "Oh, he won a nomination, oh, surprise! And now [he] can raise money so easily because his dad is a big wheel in [his] community," Brown said.

It's true that in some cases the party didn't meddle, or wasn't present at all. And some individuals opted to disregard direct orders from federal party headquarters and got away with it. We've already mentioned Liberal John Godfrey, for instance, who had in the months leading up to the 1993 election been campaigning in Markham–Whitchurch-Stouffville and not really getting anywhere. When he heard that the Liberal candidate in Don Valley West was stepping down, he called a party advisor and asked whether he could transfer his candidacy to Don Valley West. The advisor told him to wait until the leader returned from holiday. "I said, uh uh, I am not going to wait. I am just going to do this," Godfrey said. "I will ask your permission afterwards. . . . We got the hell out of Markham–Whitchurch-Stouffville, jumped over [to Don Valley West] and started signing up members," he said. So while the other potential candidates poked around, exploring the potential of a candidacy, Godfrey and his wife were selling memberships. Enough, eventually, to deter any competition.

"We started setting up memberships while the party was

still exploring possible candidates," said Godfrey. "I sold enough memberships to scare off others. . . . I didn't ask permission of Mr. Chrétien to run. I just said I am doing it." Godfrey ended up getting himself elected as the MP for Don Valley West, which he represented for the next fifteen years until his retirement from politics in 2010.

CRITICISM OF THE nomination process was strikingly common among participants in the Samara exit interviews—and they were the people who had navigated it successfully. We cringe to imagine what those who were less successful might say. When it's the winner of a race who complains about the rules of the competition, that competition itself could certainly benefit from greater scrutiny.

The nomination process should be a chance to closely explore and debate issues that are important to the community that the candidates hope to serve in Ottawa. A few MPs mentioned positive aspects of the nomination process: it was a practice round for the actual election, and it helped challenge and polish the contenders' views. A few others pointed out that nomination races, which by their nature tend to be contested among people with similar values, allowed candidates to explore finer details of community issues and policies, exchanging ideas with each other and with local party members.

But at its worst, the nomination process is a manifestation of the negative perceptions that people tend to have of politics—an opaque, manipulative and even cruel game that turns both citizens and candidates away from the democratic process. The process can be confusing, mysterious and inconsistent. As many Canadians suspect, the inner workings are subject to manipulation by riding associations, the national leadership of a party and local groups.

So what measures could improve things? A greater respect for the nomination process on the part of political parties, for one. More opportunities for genuine input from party local members. Fewer parachuted-in candidates. More transparency from the central party and local associations on how nominations run, and how citizens can participate. More advance notice of the contests, with clear processes, preferably outlined online for anyone to see, explaining how to become a candidate. More opportunities for new members to engage with the concerns of the party they've just joined. More nomination battles that are truly contested at the riding level, and fewer that are controlled by the parties' interests. In sum, more nomination battles that resemble Monte Solberg's, and fewer that resemble Omar Alghabra's. Respecting the democratic component of the nomination process means recognizing that the process itself is a valuable and important way to engage citizens in the business of running their country.

A good nomination has the power to inspire. It provides a sense of investment in the successful candidate and ownership of the position he or she occupies, as Monte Solberg's constituents were proud to have experienced. A well-run nomination battle is excellent marketing for politics itself. Few processes in politics provide such an opportunity to attract newcomers. The parties need to recognize that the opposite also holds true: nothing repels newcomers to the arena more than a nomination process that feels murky or shady, a poignant acknowledgment that even in Canada's democracy, politics can be little more than a backroom game.

CHAPTER THREE

. . . Into the Fire

The idiosyncratic nomination process is only the first of several difficult rites of passage in a prospective MP's journey to Parliament Hill. Especially for the first-time candidate, the campaign can be gruelling. And the learning curve facing every rookie MP presents its own set of challenges. Among the many MPs who offered us insight into both passages was Gary Merasty, from the Pelican Narrows Indian Reserve in northeastern Saskatchewan. Merasty belonged to the reserve's first generation for whom post-secondary education was considered an option. Born in 1964, the stocky and spectacled full-status member of the Cree Nation played hockey for a year after high school, took an industrial mechanics course and then worked for three years at a mine in Flin Flon, just over the Manitoba border. Then he went to the University of Saskatchewan for a Bachelor of Education degree, and returned home to teach in Pelican Narrows. He taught for seven years, and then turned his attention to politics, becoming a well-regarded two-term grand chief of the Prince Albert Grand Council.

Federal politics beckoned in 2005. The federal Liberal party had been cultivating Merasty as a potential candidate for some time. They even took the extraordinary step of bringing to Ottawa all the chiefs Merasty represented as grand chief so that Prime Minister Paul Martin could reassure them of the good that Merasty could do in the federal government. The measure won the chiefs' support, and on December 2, Merasty was acclaimed as his riding's Liberal nominee. Election day was less than two months away, on January 23, 2006.

Merasty's riding of Desnethé–Missinippi–Churchill River is almost as large as Germany. It encompasses the whole of Saskatchewan's northern half. To campaign, Merasty drove through early winter's blowing snow and over black ice, cruising across the arrow-straight rural roads in a Toyota 4Runner with his wife, Brenda, and his campaign manager, Bonnie Leask. And then he set out on his strategy: he thought of his riding as 70 percent aboriginal and 30 percent non-aboriginal. He was battling a Conservative incumbent. Not an aboriginal. Thanks to the goodwill Merasty had built up as a grand chief, he had the advantage. If, that is, everyone who was eligible to cast a ballot turned out to vote.

The problem, as Merasty knew, was that First Nations tended not to vote in federal and provincial elections. "The 30 percent non-aboriginal show up to vote in high numbers, typically, and the aborginals don't," he explained. His challenge? Mobilize the 70 percent.

Merasty knew that the tribal council elections on the province's reserves could attract voter participation rates of 95 percent. They participated in the democratic process. They just didn't participate in federal democracy. "It's not that they're not political," said Merasty. "It's just the relevance— they didn't feel the federal government was relevant to them."

Nor did they feel the federal government was particularly sympathetic to their problems. And there were others, like Merasty's own mother, who could remember needing the federal government's permission to leave the reserve; it was 1960 before the federal government had even granted Status Indians the unconditional right to vote.

So how to make federal politics matter to the aboriginals of northern Saskatchewan? Merasty started with Pelican Narrows, where typically only a couple of hundred voted out of the fifteen hundred who were eligible. "Your vote matters," he told them. "Only 15–20 percent of you are voting. But First Nations could decide the outcome."

The populace was too sparsely distributed for Merasty to reach everyone. He relied on contacting the movers and shakers on each reserve, then trusted them to distribute his message to everyone else. One typical visit happened at Cumberland House in northeastern Saskatchewan, where Merasty sat down with Chief Lorne Stewart and his tribal council.

"You try and convince them that the role of an MP and MLA is important and it helps shape the future and their participation in the future," he said. At community gatherings in school gyms, Merasty took questions from the audience. "Why should we worry about voting," one man asked, "when we don't have jobs?" Another said, "Who cares about voting— get us some more housing. Our houses are too crowded." The gist of what Merasty heard was that voting is a waste of time.

"I agree—government has not been helpful," Merasty responded. "You see the evidence of that when you see twenty people living in a three-bedroom house. And when the educational spending on a First Nations child is one-third less than what it is elsewhere in the province." But if the First Nations turned out to vote, Merasty said, they could elect one of their own to represent them. And if Merasty made it to Ottawa, then he'd work inside the system to try to fix those problems. "I don't dispute the problems you're mentioning," Merasty said at Cumberland House. "But the power of your vote is loud."

In reserve community centres, in school gyms, huddled into tiny kitchens, Merasty repeated his message. What he remembers most about that period is the darkness. It would start to get dark around four in the afternoon, and once he finished delivering his message it was back into the 4Runner for another long drive through the dark and the cold to the next reservation town, where he'd do it all again. He campaigned in places where no one had ever campaigned before—places the other candidates thought too small, places everyone else dismissed because the Indians didn't vote anyway. During the eight-week campaign he and his wife and campaign manager put 30,000 kilometres on their SUV.

That last week Merasty reminded his supporters: Get out. Vote. Bring government-issued photo ID, and if you don't have that, then bring three pieces of mail. The week before the election, it was minus 38 degrees Celsius, but luckily election day was positively balmy—the mercury actually topped zero. That evening, when the polls closed, Merasty was in Creighton, just down the road from Flin Flon, watching the television at RJ's Motel. The numbers were close. Merasty led, he trailed, he led, and when the tally finally came in, he had won by 10,225 to 10,119, a margin of just 106 votes. The Conservative incumbent, Jeremy Harrison, challenged the result, alleging, among other things, that the Ahtahkakoop First Nation had staged a raffle for a television on election night, in a gambit designed to get out the vote. Another alleged irregularity involved a box of ballots that had somehow ended up being used as insulation for the grill of a pick-up truck. After a judge-ordered recount, Merasty held on to his victory, albeit with the margin narrowed to sixty-seven votes.

According to Merasty, the First Nations vote went up by 25 percent over previous elections. Merasty was the first full-status aboriginal person from the province of Saskatchewan to make it to the House of Commons. It had been a bumpy ride (literally!): a last-minute nomination, a gruelling election campaign, a contested result. He'd survived one roller coaster, only to find that another lay ahead.

AFTER ANY FEDERAL ELECTION, roughly a third of our Members of Parliament arrive on the steps of Parliament's Centre Block as rookies. They emerge victorious from an often-difficult nomination battle and general election campaign. They come from a wide variety of backgrounds, and bring with them a diverse set of experiences and motives, but unlike Merasty, they often arrive with little—if any—experience in elected office or in the context of national public life.

How did these self-described accidental politicians feel once they first arrived in Ottawa? And how did they navigate those initial weeks and months in office? We hadn't expected our MPs' vivid recollections of nomination battles so long ago fought, and we were just as surprised by their tales of the rude awakening that greeted them in Ottawa.

Virtually all the MPs we interviewed remembered feeling, immediately, two powerful emotions. First, they were filled with awe for the institution of Parliament and its history, and for the opportunity to serve, believing that they were part of something important and ready for the challenge. And then there was a double take at being left to fend for themselves.

Take Marlene Catterall, a teacher and former Ottawa city councillor who became a Liberal MP in 1988, representing the riding of Ottawa West. When Catterall walked into the House of Commons for the first time, she looked around at the oak panelling, the ceiling painted with the provincial emblems, the stained glass windows at which so many other federal politicians had also gazed, and she thought, "What a great country they've given us." What a great country—and she felt what others had felt: the call to continue that greatness, to make sure it was a better country once she left the House of Commons. "To be one of only 308 people chosen from the entire population of this country," she thought. "How much more of an honour could you possibly have?"

"It's awe-inspiring," recalled Art Hanger, a former Calgary policeman turned Reform MP who first went to the House of Commons in 1993. "This is no frivolous position that you have. . . . It's ultra-important, you're representing the people of this nation and you have a responsibility, a substantial responsibility, and you'd better do it right."

Many MPs shared similar sentiments. "All I can say is, very exciting," recalled Victoria Liberal David Anderson, first elected in 1968. "We were all ushered in, and there was Trudeau. It was tremendous. It's a beautiful room. The carving, the velvet drapery, it's a beautiful room."

While the sense of responsibility and history inspired them, the MPs were startled to find how little help there was for them after they arrived. It felt a little duplicitous, this aspect of the political career. The party that, in many cases, had pleaded with the candidates to run in the election, approved their nominations and whose logos adorned their lawn signs, now was proving itself anything but supportive. In fact, with the MPs now firmly positioned in their political careers, and almost trapped in Ottawa, the parties (no matter which one) repeatedly showed themselves to be apathetic about how the newcomers fared in nearly all aspects of their jobs. Except for one: how they vote. During the first few days in Ottawa, MPs experience their first inkling that the party doesn't value them as much as they'd thought. It's at this point that new MPs realize they're on their own—and sometimes painfully so.

Following the 1993 election, over 72 percent of the MPs were rookies, the largest class of freshman MPs in modern Canadian history. Audiences tuning in to the evening news were treated to an indelible symbol of their bewilderment, as a CTV camera crew followed Reform MP Myron Thompson through his first day of the parliamentary session. Born in the United States, Thompson had tried out for the New York Yankees and served in the U.S. Army before moving to Canada in 1968. He had been a teacher, a school principal and the mayor of his town before becoming the MP for the Wild Rose riding in southwestern Alberta. At one point that first day on Parliament Hill he set down his briefcase in the House of Commons, removed some papers and then became distracted. A bit later, as he was about to leave the Chamber, he picked up the same briefcase and all his papers went flying—he'd forgotten to close the clasp. The same day, with the camera crew still tagging along, Thompson was heading from one parliamentary building to another when a shuttle bus drove up alongside him and the driver leaned out to offer him a ride. "I was looking at [the driver] and I stepped off the curb and didn't see what was there, and I stumbled and nearly broke my neck," Thompson recalls. "Of course I was the main feature on the news that night."

Thompson's pratfalls publicly illustrated how many other MPs felt. "I was so frightened when I won," recalls Colleen Beaumier, a Liberal MP who, like Thompson, also went to the House for the first time in 1993. "When I got there we had our orientation and I sat on the steps of the Peace Tower, and Paul Szabo [also newly elected] came out and said, 'Colleen, what are you crying for? We've been wanting this for years.' And I said, 'No, this isn't something I always wanted. Such beautiful people supported me and I'm going to disappoint them.'"

Fear of failure and lack of confidence are typical for freshmen MPs in Canada, as they apparently are in Britain, where the Parliamentary Library's most-borrowed book is the instructional manual for new politicians: *How To Be an MP*. The fact that some Canadian MPs had never even visited Parliament before intensified their initial insecurity. "The learning curve was steep," recalls Blair Wilson, who began sitting in 2006 as a Liberal MP, and who, after allegations of omissions on his nomination application, finished his time in Parliament as a member of the Green Party. "I learned quickly but I have to say that I knew very little about how the actual mechanism of Ottawa worked. I had never been there. . . . The very first time I walked up to the door of the House of Commons was after I was elected as a Member of Parliament."

Rick Casson, the former MP for Lethbridge, Alberta, a safe Conservative seat, remembers talking to his wife about what he'd just gotten them into as they drove home from his nomination victory. "Jeanene and I had a couple of conversations after we won the nomination. . . . I said: 'What the hell are we doing now?' And she said: 'Well, I don't know. I guess we'll find out.' So the night after we got elected for the general election, [we] said the same thing . . . we had no idea," he recalled. He'd been involved in politics municipally, so knew how things worked in southern Alberta. But Ottawa? Not so much. "We didn't have anything to do with the federal government," he said. "Our MLA would come and see us once or twice a year. But the MP? Never."

Fredericton Liberal and Cabinet member Andy Scott admitted to feeling "overwhelmed" when he first sat in the House of Commons, and "naïve." He connected the feeling to another attitude we mentioned earlier, saying, "I grew up modestly and never aspired to any of this stuff. I wasn't one of those people who was thinking about this when I was twelve." (Andy Scott died in June 2013.)

The new parliamentarians' adjustment to public life was made more difficult by the dearth of structured orientation to help them acclimatize to their new roles. At an orientation day conducted by parliamentary staff after the election and before the first day the House sits, the bare necessities, such as how to file expenses, are explained. But most of the MPs we interviewed felt the orientation was nowhere near sufficient. "You get there, they take you in the House, they give you a book [on] constituency rights and responsibilities, the former Speaker talks about being in the House, and that's it," said

Reg Alcock, a Winnipeg-area Liberal MP first elected in 1993. "There's no orientation. There is no training. There is nothing on how to be effective."

The political parties certainly didn't offer much by way of support. Rick Casson, an Alberta MP first elected in 1997 in the second wave of Reform MPs, found his initial days jolting. "The biggest surprise that I had when I went down there after being elected through the Reform Party was the total . . . I had some ideas about this big, well-greased machine [but] it was chaos. It was crazy," he said. "I don't know what it would have been like in '93, when they all went down there. I went there in '97, and at least they had a few years under the belt. But, as far as being new and thinking that somehow, there's going to be some leadership or that someone is going to take you by the hand or whatever, there was none of that. . . . You are on your own."

Whatever preparation the new parliamentarians did manage was largely ad hoc and really began only once they arrived in Ottawa. "You learn by the seat of your pants," observed Claudette Bradshaw, a Liberal from New Brunswick. "I was always amazed at how people go into it without having done any kind of homework," said the NDP's Penny Priddy. And Myron Thompson argued that by the time MPs arrived in Ottawa, it was already too late. "[Orientation] should take place long before the election. . . . Find out what the heck you're getting into before you ever decide to run," he said.

Marlene Catterall observed that there was no opportunity to set goals or develop a plan. "It would be very wise to have someone encourage you to sit down at the beginning and say, 'Okay, what is it you want to accomplish?' It is such a busy life, you just tend to jump in and keep swimming. You should almost have to go on a retreat to think through what it is you want to accomplish," she said.

Many MPs sought informal advice and mentorship, but found that even that wasn't always helpful. "You're getting tugged in every which way by different advice, so it was pretty confusing when we were first there," said Toronto Liberal MP Bill Graham. Even more experienced parliamentarians weren't always able to provide direction. Catherine Bell recalled asking for advice from a colleague. "He said, 'I don't know; I've been here for three years and I really don't know.' And I thought, 'Gosh. . . . It takes a long time to learn things.'"

Some found their fellow MPs less than supportive. "Guys are really protective of their knowledge because of the ladder climbers; they won't share and . . . they don't want you to become as smart as they think they are. Even in the same party. If I have a little more information than you, then I got a better chance," Casson said.

One exception to this overall lack of guidance was that of the new Bloc Québécois MPs to whom we spoke, many of whom were assigned a party mentor upon their arrival. They were grateful for the help. "I had a good MP as a mentor," said Alain Boire, a Bloc MP for Beauharnois–Salaberry. "He had been there for a long time. . . . I asked for his advice often. I didn't even know that when the bell rang I was supposed to enter the Chamber. I didn't know that; I didn't know anything." However, the Bloc's mentoring program seemed not to be universal, since other Bloc MPs explicitly mentioned that they would have benefited from mentorship.

Only a few MPs said they spent time learning parliamentary rules and procedure. "Robert's Rules of Order, all those books were there, I read them, I learned them, I sat and watched other people, and I didn't participate much in the beginning. I really just absorbed," said Liberal MP Sue Barnes. Meanwhile, her fellow MP, David Anderson, pointed out that it was rare for his colleagues to engage in that kind of preparation. "Next to nobody knows the rules of the House," Anderson said.

Even apart from the rules, many newcomers claimed to have had little or no knowledge of the methods, traditions or culture of Parliament. This was particularly the case for those elected as members of the Reform Party. "Fifty-one of us went and didn't know a damned thing about the House of Commons. . . . [We were like] deer in the headlights," admitted Randy White, a member of the initial group of Reform MPs.

Many soon realized they had no sense of the complex rules and processes—both written and unwritten—of Parliament Hill, or how to navigate a place where so many divergent personalities and issues come together. It was difficult to see the pattern. For some, the challenge came from the realization that they lacked a broad knowledge of the country and its regional idiosyncrasies. "I was naïve, thinking this place has three hundred people and that they can all work together on global problems. . . . That wasn't the case at all," said White.

Many had moments not unlike that described by Barry Campbell, a backbench MP who sat as a rookie in the 35th Parliament of 1993. "We were First Nations, new Canadians, Ph.D.s, historians, teachers, store clerks, former CEOs, lawyers, yes, but also a convicted criminal, and, I would soon discover, the mentally certifiable," Campbell wrote in an adroit series for the *Walrus* about his experience as an MP in 2008. "For some, this was the best job they'd ever had; for others, it would be the worst. For some, the parliamentary salary was the most money they had ever earned; for others, the least. There were single mothers and divorced fathers. . . . It was a community gathering, a microcosm of Canada."

Said Liberal MP Andy Mitchell, "You tend to understand where you come from really well, and you think of reality through that prism. All of a sudden you are in Parliament. You are working with men and women from right across the country, who all come from a different prism." Others mentioned being overwhelmed by the volume of work and the range of policy files they had to understand, usually very quickly. "Despite all the people that advised me, I had no clue as to what I was getting myself into . . . the biggest surprises were the demands placed upon you. There weren't enough hours in a day. There never would be," said Liberal MP Paul Macklin.

The extent of this pressure should not be a surprise; following an election, federal politicians begin work almost immediately after the ballots are counted and little time remains for orientation or acclimatization. On top of it all, there are the logistical challenges. For many parliamentarians, Ottawa is an unfamiliar city, often a long flight away from friends and family, and they need to find a place to live and sort out family arrangements.

MPs also must immediately set up and staff at least two offices—one in Ottawa and one or more in the riding— and orient themselves to the labyrinth of Parliament Hill and the federal government writ large. A number of MPs mentioned that they had little or no experience hiring staff and managing an office, and found little support in doing so.

"There are a few areas in which MPs bring very little experience to the Hill [including] how to run an office, how to hire people and how to look for [particular] skills," observed Marlene Catterall.

Even MPs with prior experience in provincial or municipal government found the initial weeks and months difficult. Penny Priddy, for instance, who'd previously served as a municipal councillor and a provincial Cabinet minister in B.C., said it was "incredibly difficult" to get started operationally. "There was just so much that I didn't know. I was very frustrated at not being up and running as quickly as I thought I should be, which of course is always yesterday," she said.

In the end, many MPs simply accepted that there was just no way to be prepared for day one as a Member of Parliament. "Well, I think we all did rather well. But were we prepared?" asked an NDP MP from Winnipeg, Bill Blaikie. "No, I don't think there is any school for preparation for being a Member of Parliament." Muskoka Liberal Andy Mitchell agreed: "If you could arrive at Parliament knowing the way it works and all of those things, then you [would] be more productive from day one. But that's theoretical; it's never going to happen that way."

Instead, the MPs acknowledged that the learning curve was daunting, and that the only way forward was to learn by doing. "In the first days of Reform, the big class of '93, our learning curve was vertical," recalls B.C. MP Jim Gouk. "Literally, we had nobody to tell us anything. Plus, [even from] the little that people could tell us—we were down there to try it differently. So we made lots of mistakes." Likewise, Liberal MP Roger Galloway said: "It takes time to figure out how it works . . . and [to figure out] what I want to do here. What can I do here? You don't do that in a month, or a year. It's an evolution over time."

THE FAMILIES OF MPs are of course tossed into the fray as well. Galloway left behind a wife and four young children in the Sarnia area when he first went to Ottawa as an MP in 1993, and he made the weekly commute to Ottawa and back for the five-or-so months a year that Parliament is in session. "It's not the big events you miss at home, being away," Galloway said. "It's the day-to-day rhythm that's affected."

The challenge for the families of commuting MPs is even greater than missing out on that daily rhythm of family life. What came through in our interviews was the personal sacrifice that serving as a federal politician also entails, particularly when considering the strains on relationships with spouses, children and other loved ones. Galloway noted that his four children occasionally bore the brunt of his public profile in snide comments from others, including their teachers. "It's tough for the kids," Galloway said. "Because old people make comments about your father. . . . All of a sudden you are in the public eye."

The personal cost of political life was a subject that recurred again and again in the interviews, unbidden. And it was through such references to the strains that political life brought to MPs' families and friends that we began to appreciate what a sacrifice MPs were making—the grinding commutes, the missed birthdays, abbreviated family vacations and declined social invitations, the inevitable tension in personal relationships.

A paper about MPs' difficulty in achieving a work-life balance, co-authored by Alison Loat and political scientists Royce Koop and James Farney, mentions the high toll of political life on family life. It cites the consideration, chronicled in Steve Paikin's *The Dark Side* and much discussed elsewhere, that many MPs will either be divorced or will have done serious damage to their marriages by the end of their political careers.

"The time away from your family is a lot," said Blair Wilson, an MP from B.C. "I look at some of these people who just got elected and have young families and you don't realize what you are missing. So that is why we should give them even more support because that's what they're giving up to represent us."

"It's very hard for a woman," said the Conservative MP for Saskatoon–Rosetown–Biggar, Carol Skelton. "I find that I don't know how people with young children do it. I really don't. When I was down there, I was worried about my kids, and they're all older." Skelton had three grown children and credits the tolerance and support of her husband, Noel, a farmer, with allowing her to pursue the job as she did. "He was very understanding and put up with a lot, because you're gone all the time," Skelton said. "He was the full-time farmer, and we had livestock, so he didn't come to Ottawa. When I did come home, it was also very busy. I really missed those years with my family because of the distance between Ottawa and Saskatchewan."

Parliamentarians who had to commute to Newfoundland or B.C., or northern ridings, described gruelling schedules. And whether an MP had grown or young children, or any children at all, tended to affect the extent of the personal sacrifice. "I always considered myself fortunate," said Liberal MP for Etobicoke North, Roy Cullen. "My house was close to the airport, so I could be on a six o'clock flight out of Ottawa and I'd actually be in my home at quarter to eight. Where some of these people have to travel, I don't know how they do it . . . If you have a young family and the wife's not working and you're living in B.C., I mean, frankly I don't know how they cope."

And even though air travel made it possible to come home most weekends and the weeks were busy, downtime in Ottawa could sometimes be hard to fill. Rick Casson from Lethbridge made a few notes before his interview to remind himself of what he wanted to say. "I wrote down 'important.' Because I do feel that being a Member of Parliament is very important . . . but one other word I wrote down is 'lonely,' because it can be pretty damn lonely down there. . . . There are a lot of nights when you are alone in the apartment and that's it. The first year I stayed in a hotel, it was absolutely horrific. . . . Getting an apartment was the best thing to do, and then Jeanene retired after about five years, so that made a hell of a lot of difference. Having her come down was great, it would give you something to look forward to, to go home. But other than that, you leave the office at 7 p.m. to go home; what the hell do you do? That's where guys get in trouble, if they don't go home. That's when they get in trouble."

SO HOW DID Gary Merasty fare in a workplace that provides little orientation and less work-life balance? Although a newcomer to Parliament, recall that Merasty was an experienced political operator, previously serving as a two-term grand chief of the Indian peoples of central and northern Saskatchewan, 34,000 in all, who points to his having expanded the programs offered by the band he governed from $28 million to $52 million in the six years he served as chief. He also recalled his response while a grand chief to a statistic used by the federal government that indicated it would take twenty-eight years for testing results of First Nations kids to catch up to the Canadian average. His band government began collecting its own statistics. For example, Merasty directed his staff to begin tracking graduation rates at the fifteen high schools under the Grand Council's purview. In 1998 they discovered that only 34 percent of the students graduated from grade 12. As a former teacher himself, Merasty made it his mission to raise the rate, and six years later, the graduation rate had risen to 92 percent. Merasty was a savvy operator, an adept politician accustomed to succeeding at problems other people found intractable.

And yet in Ottawa, even he found it difficult to hit the ground running. Even he felt overwhelmed. Like many new MPs, Merasty scheduled his first visit to Ottawa after the election to coincide with the Liberal Party's first caucus meeting. He arrived and received his office assignment from the party whip—room 714 in the Confederation Building. He slowly found his way there, passing many other people wearing similarly lost expressions.

The work began immediately and the workdays proved intense—day-long House sessions, committee meetings with fellow MPs, meetings with constituents and associations, fulfilling party duties and trying to stay on top of correspondence. Though their workdays are full, most MPs generally attend fewer sessions in the House of Commons than many citizens realize: typically, they're in the House only for

Question Period, votes and a few hours of weekly House Duty, as assigned to them by their party whips.

And for Merasty, a change of priorities was in order. He'd gone in expecting the Liberals to form the government. But Paul Martin's party won only 103 seats to the 124 taken by Stephen Harper's Conservatives; the Liberals were relegated to the other side of the house. That forced Merasty to reconsider his goals. "Our goal in opposition was to take the government to task on aboriginal issues and I knew them inside and out," Merasty recalls. "Two was to educate my own party about the aboriginal issues and three was, what can we do to increase the aboriginal vote?"

Even then, when he arrived, he found he was absorbed less by grand strategies than by the nitty-gritty details that consume many people when they start a new job. What support would he need to succeed? Whom would he hire to staff his office? How many? And how much should he pay them? The questions seemed insurmountable. "I didn't have a clear idea of what type of person I should hire to run my office. What are their day-to-day tasks?" Merasty recalled wondering.

What saved him was a thirteen-page letter circulated by Paul Szabo, by then a veteran Liberal MP. The thirteen pages were chock full of advice expressly intended as a public service to assist freshmen MPs like Merasty. Did he wonder about staffing offices? Szabo had thought of that: "Most MPs have four or five staff split between Ottawa and their constituency office," his letter explains. "I personally have only one office assistant in Ottawa and three persons in the riding to do constituency work at a total cost of less than $170,000 [. . . .] There are no votes for you in Ottawa and therefore your best staff should be in the riding to take care of the needs of your constituents. . . . The best thing you can do is make sure you have at least two solid people in the riding and a comfortable, spacious, well-equipped office."

Szabo's advice was detailed, pragmatic and succinct. He also gave Merasty some advice in person. As Merasty recalled it: "Nobody will coach you because they are all competing to be in Cabinet at some point or have this appointment later on and so everyone is clawing up. So you have to trust your team—but be aware of that dynamic. . . . be aware of the partisanship, and just be true to yourself."

The guidance was just what Merasty needed. Also helpful was the fact that the only other Liberal MP from Saskatchewan was a high-ranking party member, the former finance minister and Liberal House leader Ralph Goodale.

On Merasty's first day as a sitting parliamentarian— April 3, 2006—the first substantive order of business saw the most veteran sitting member of the House, the NDP MP from the riding of Elmwood–Transcona, Bill Blaikie, presiding over the election of the Speaker of the House—Liberal MP Peter Milliken. And as Merasty watched the proceedings, he was awed.

He still sounds awestruck as he recalls the first time he rose as an MP and addressed the House. "It was really one of those moments in life that you always remember—at least for me it certainly was—the chance to be able to rise in Canada's Parliament and to speak directly to my constituents and to Canadians and of course, you take the opportunity to thank the folks that helped you arrive there; whether they be your campaign team, whether it be your family, it's important to recognize nobody arrives in Parliament by themselves. They arrive as a part of a team. They arrive as a result of the efforts of others. They are there because their family is supporting them to be there. So it was an important thing to do that as well. It was an exciting moment. . . . When you say something in the House it's there forever. It's in Hansard forever. A hundred years from now, not that anybody will, but if somebody so chose—my great-great-great-grandchild might decide, 'Hey, I didn't know my great-great-great-grandfather was in Parliament. Let me just look something up here.' And it's there."

Merasty received committee assignments for aboriginal affairs and agriculture. He became the Liberal Party's associate critic on Indian Affairs. He attacked the Conservative government's apparent apathy concerning the Kelowna Accord, the 2005 agreement between Paul Martin's federal government, provincial and territorial premiers, and First Nations leaders.

But Merasty said his biggest success on the First Nations front concerned residential schools, the educational institutions that from 1874 until the mid-1970s had forcibly separated aboriginal children from their families and communities and placed them in the care of religious institutions, where many of them were sexually and physically abused; many more were subject to overcrowded conditions, substandard sanitation and poor health care that made them susceptible to such diseases as tuberculosis. A legal settlement that provided funds to approximately 86,000 residential school survivors was in the process of being approved by provincial and territorial courts throughout 2006 and into 2007. The compensation was monetary; it didn't involve any government apology. This irked Merasty, whose mother was a residential school survivor, as were relatives and friends. "I know the history," Merasty told us. "I know that hundreds, if not thousands, of kids died in these residential schools, buried in snowbanks until the ground thawed in the summer until they could be buried in unmarked graves that we still don't know where they are." Merasty referred to his relatives the first time he stood up in the House to ask the government for an apology, on November 7, 2006. "On behalf of my mother, my aunts, my uncles and my community, when will the prime minister offer a simple human apology to the survivors of the residential school?" he asked.

Merasty worked on the issue through the early months of 2007. The gist of the government's position, Merasty felt, was that residential schools weren't that bad; that they'd been intended for education. In April 2007, he wrote a letter to Jim Prentice, the Conservative Indian Affairs minister, raising the residential schools issue and pointing out that the abuse wasn't just physical or sexual but also involved the government's putting aboriginal children at increased risk of severe illness. The media began quoting him as a source on the issue. Working behind the scenes, Merasty won the support of his party for a motion calling on the House of Commons to apologize. The NDP also would support him, he learned. And then on the morning that he was to make the motion, on April 30, the Conservatives decided they'd also support it. Later that day, when he rose in the House to introduce the motion, Merasty painted a vivid portrait of the schools' effects: "I stand here for numerous victims whose stories will never be told, whose remains are scattered across our land in unmarked graves, scars on the land and even larger scars on our nation's psyche." The motion passed unanimously, 257 to zero—a remarkable success for a rookie MP.

Meanwhile, however, the Liberal Party was in the midst of a transition period, attempting to rebound in the face of the Conservative Party's rise. Leader Paul Martin stepped down, and in the resulting leadership race, Merasty backed Michael Ignatieff—who, in that round at least, would come in second to the eventual winner, Stéphane Dion.

In July 2007, only sixteen months after he was elected, Merasty announced his resignation from Parliament, effective that August. In the press release, Merasty insisted he supported Dion; he said family obligations to his wife and four children played the biggest role in his departure. Asked what made the job difficult, Gary Merasty responded promptly: "Family." Then continued: "Because we had a seven-year-old and the older kids helped out, but it's tough on family . . . it was a little worse than I thought. My wife was supportive to the end . . . but it was a family issue. And perhaps feeling guilty a bit through my six years as grand chief and my sixteen-year-old—well now she's sixteen, when I was there she was about thirteen—but you missed a whole lot. . . . And then I went to be an MP and I thought, 'Hmm, am I going to do this to my then five-year-old?'"

Health also was a factor, he said. But in his exit interview, he also cited a job offer from the private sector as a major factor in the resignation—a job that "was to have a more on-the-ground, immediate impact" in Merasty's aboriginal community. The job was the vice-president of corporate and social responsibility for Cameco, a global uranium mining firm with a major presence in northern Saskatchewan. That a former Cree grand chief felt that he could do more for the First Nations population of northern Saskatchewan in the private sector than in Parliament is a disturbing indictment of our country's federal political system and its failure to take advantage of the gifts of a man who had been identified as "one of the top next-generation leaders in the party."

Merasty's resignation had more to do with party politics and considerations for his young family than it did with a poor parliamentary orientation process. Nevertheless, he was a detail-oriented, self-described "data geek" who professed to be baffled by an MP's job. With the help of Paul Szabo, Ralph Goodale and others in his party, Merasty learned enough to help reverse the residential schools policy of a Conservative government of which he was not a part. That even Merasty felt unprepared in his early days suggests that we can improve on the way newly elected parliamentarians are prepared for their positions.

Several recent efforts have provided new or aspiring politicians with more education, including initiatives from Carleton University to welcome the rookie MPs after the 2011 election, enhancements to the Library of Parliament's orientation and a "boot camp" run by the University of British Columbia for people considering a run for office. Efforts to provide training to parliamentarians have come and gone over the years. Let's hope these ideas continue to gain currency among aspiring and serving politicians. Despite these recent efforts, it remains hard to disagree with Paul Szabo's observations to Gary Merasty that "nobody will coach you" and "everyone is clawing up." And with an average of a hundred MPs making their debut after each election, nearly a third of Parliament is basically being thrown into the deep end.

In the House of Commons, where an atmosphere of mutual support and education would enable our MPs to do their job better, it's unfortunate that a collegial willingness by a veteran to help a freshman is so rare. Would it be possible for the experienced MPs to institute a regular, more substantive orientation for newly elected MPs? High-performing organizations in the private, non-profit and public sectors, or those that aspire to be, all invest heavily in orientation, executive education and ongoing coaching. That high level of support stands in direct contrast to the lack of support measures in Canadian politics. The cursory nature of the orientation process for MPs is a clear indication that they are undervalued and that political leaders regard them as little more than votes. That their veteran colleagues don't want to help them do their jobs—and that their own parties don't seem to care whether they are able to represent their constituents effectively or hold government to account—may be the starkest possible indication of the failure of our party politics, and of the troubled future of our democracy.

CHAPTER FOUR

What Job Is This Anyway?

Once they've faced down the challenges of their first weeks in Ottawa—where the office is, how to claim expenses, where to find staff, how to get to the bathroom—new MPs face a more long-term hurdle: managing the many demands on their attention and schedule. The former Liberal MP for Miramichi, New Brunswick, Charles Hubbard, for one, was astonished by the number of people who approached his office to seek help from one of the federal bureaucracies, such as Immigration Canada, Revenue Canada or Service Canada. "Your office is always facing calls where somebody is frustrated with trying to approach the government," said Hubbard. "When you think of somebody having trouble with his income tax or with his EI or trying to access the Canada Pension or an old age pension, and they get the proverbial runaround, they wind up calling your office."

In fact, Hubbard's office dealt with this type of matter so frequently that he assigned the equivalent of two and a half full-time people to handle the calls (most MPs have only half a dozen staff between their two offices). The staffers, Hubbard said, averaged more than a hundred such calls per day; in the fifteen years that he served as an MP, Hubbard figures his staffers handled more than a hundred thousand calls that involved constituents seeking help in their dealings with federal government bureaucracies.

A high school principal before entering politics, Hubbard shared a story about a former student in desperate need of help. By then about thirty-five years old, the man had a wife and three kids, and was dying of cancer—and yet Service Canada was denying him his disability payments. When Hubbard heard about the situation he called the man's doctor, who subsequently wrote a statement to support the man's claim, which Hubbard then made sure was read by the proper person at Service Canada. A month before the former student's death, Service Canada approved the man for the disability pension. The money would make an enormous difference in the lives of the man's family—his kids would get the payments until they came of age, and his wife would get payments as long as she needed them. "So, you know, as a Member of Parliament, you have people in need who call you, and who can benefit from a bit of effort you put into it," Hubbard said.

Hubbard came to regard dealing with these appeals for help with the Canadian federal bureaucracy as an important aspect of the MP's job. When we asked which part of his work as a parliamentarian he enjoyed most, Hubbard mentioned these cases. "You probably get more satisfaction from helping people than you did from trying to wade through legislation," Hubbard said. "And the struggles in Ottawa, in terms of trying to put forward your ideas, or to get changes done, it's a very frustrating experience. And when you look at somebody who is in need of Canada Pension, who's been denied it . . . by bureaucrats who've never seen them, and the person comes to [your] office and you see the condition he's in, and he has five kids at home and is disabled and you can help that person, there's probably more satisfaction from that."

FEW WOULD EVER FAULT Charles Hubbard for doing what he could to help any individual, let alone a former student, facing such tragic circumstances. But we were struck by the number of MPs who had similar stories. Is this what voters send MPs to Ottawa to do? In our interviews, we also asked the MPs to describe their jobs. We wanted to know how they spent their time once they got settled in Ottawa, and what they learned about how to succeed as an MP. When we reviewed their descriptions of the MP's role and what they believed they'd been sent to Ottawa to do, we were taken aback by the variety of their answers.

These wide divergences pointed to an absence of any formal job description or definition of an MP's responsibilities. And the lack of any direction from parties, which typically exercise far more control over their members, made us wonder whether the higher-ups in the parties cared what the MPs were doing, as long as the they showed up for votes in the House of Commons. As long as they didn't cause trouble, the MPs were largely left to fend for themselves. Many of them began doing something we referred to as "freelancing"—developing an expertise in a topic that interested constituents or the MP but not necessarily the party leadership. Without direction from the party that controlled many other aspects of their conduct, the MPs drifted into tasks that fell well outside what we might ever have imagined their responsibilities to be.

———

According to Canada's Library of Parliament, an MP in the Westminster system of government has three traditional roles. The first is to consider, refine and pass legislation; in other words, to establish policy and pass laws. The second is to hold government accountable for its administration of the laws and to authorize the expenditure of required funds; that is, to ensure that the laws are being carried out properly, and that tax dollars are being spent responsibly. The third role is to determine the life of the government by providing or withholding support—voting for bills you favour and voting against those you don't.

None of the MPs in our group described their jobs in terms consistent with the traditional Westminster definition, and only a few were even close. Gary Merasty was the only former MP to acknowledge that he had a problem defining an MP's job responsibility. During his campaign in December 2005 and January 2006, First Nations voters on the Saskatchewan reserves asked him a question that others, more informed of federal politics, might not have thought to ask: "What does an MP *actually* do?" What is illuminating is that Merasty was a bit stumped. He knew the broad-strokes answer—in fact, he thought of the job as requiring three different hats. "Battle hard for your constituents; be available to respond and advocate for them as much as you can," he says. "Two, you have a responsibility to this country as well; be involved in the national and international policy debates. And three, advocate for your party."

But in detail, hour by hour? "As far as really knowing what an MP does, I'd go on the website and look at the committee work and see all that. [For] work in the riding, [I'd] look at different MP websites and try to figure out what a day was like. I couldn't understand all that," Merasty recalls. "My experience leading to Ottawa was that you should have a clear understanding of what an MP does. But even when I explained it to people, I didn't [entirely] know . . . and [when I asked others], I didn't get a clear answer."

University textbooks reflect this confusion. "The concept of political representation is misleadingly simple: everyone seems to know what it is, yet few can agree on any particular definition," says Professor Suzanne Dovi in the *Stanford Encyclopedia of Philosophy*. Despite divergences, however, when we asked MPs to describe how they conceived of their roles, two broad categories emerged.

Many of the MPs we interviewed described their roles in ways that corresponded to two classic but competing definitions of a political representative's role: "trustees" and "delegates." According to political theory, trustees are representatives who follow their own sense of the best action to pursue. A trustee believes she was elected by the public to use her own judgment to make a decision. Meanwhile, delegates are understood to be representatives who follow the expressed preferences of their constituents, regardless of their own personal opinion. On occasions when an MP's judgment on a legislative matter differs from voter preference, assuming they can appropriately identify their constituents' view, the trustee will vote according to her own judgment, while the delegate will allow voter preference to have the ultimate say.

Among parliamentarians from the Liberals, New Democrats or the Bloc Québécois, no clear preference for the role of trustee or delegate emerged. Each of those parties had MPs in both groups, and in fact, many MPs straddled the categories.

Describing a classic trustee's conception of the job, NDP Bill Blaikie said: "My job as an MP was to do the thinking and the listening at the committee hearings and the meetings— albeit out of a certain perspective that I was up front about when I ran—and then to make judgments," Blaikie said. "The people who voted for me don't have the time to do all that. That is what I am paid to do. . . . [My constituents] will hold me accountable at elections and in between with their input with letters of criticism or support." And Paddy Torsney, a former Liberal MP for Burlington, said, "I think my job was to provide leadership. Not just reflect the discussion, but also to lead the discussion. And I think that is where people get caught up in 'No, my job is to do exactly what those people say.' . . . No, you're actually sending me there to think and bring more information back, too."

The majority of Conservative MPs, in contrast, approached their roles as delegates. Loyola Hearn describes the job in terms very similar to the word's definition. "[Voters] select you to be their representative in Ottawa, to speak for them, to vote on legislation and, in some cases, to develop legislation that they feel is wanted. Basically, to work [for their interests] and to deliver for them whatever benefits might flow," Hearn said. "All of [the constituents] can't be up there, so you're the messenger. That's the job you have. . . . You are the representative for the people in Ottawa, not Ottawa's representative to the people."

Some Liberals shared this view. Take, for example, the Waterloo-area MP Andrew Telegdi, who described his job this way: "MPs should be in Ottawa to represent their constituents. . . . Actually I found that quite attractive in the Reform

Party when they first got elected, and that was the message that they came through with. That's how they saw the role of a Member of Parliament."

Other MPs admitted that their sense of the job changed with time. "Well, certainly in the early days [of Reform] we made quite a show of saying that we were there to represent the constituency in Ottawa, not the other way around," said Conservative B.C. MP Chuck Strahl. "In the early days it was certainly aggressively constituency-based. You represent your constituency views to Ottawa, and even in the party you subsumed your own ideas." But in time he warmed to the value of the trustee approach. "It's not about getting goodies for the riding, it's about doing the right thing, and 'you know we expect you to go back there and do the right thing, not the party thing and not the expedient thing and not the politically correct thing, but tell it like it is on behalf of all of us.'"

A more nuanced view was to interpret an MP's purpose as being neither trustee nor delegate, but as seeking to balance the two. Several described the tension between reflecting constituents' views and leading the way toward or developing a broader view. "I knew I had to represent the voices of my constituents whether I agreed or not," said NDP Penny Priddy. "[But] it didn't mean I championed those causes."

At times, our former MPs expressed resentment toward colleagues who viewed the role differently. One MP suggested that those who viewed themselves solely as delegates didn't fully appreciate their job. "You're not running for councillor. You're not the alderman here. You are the ambassador to Ottawa," said Liberal MP John Godfrey. "I am not there as some kind of thoughtless representation of local views. They have chosen me and I have got to apply my best judgment to the situation and it may not always be popular with the constituents; but after all, if they wanted to have a popularity contest or they wanted to poll, they wouldn't need an MP. I mean you're actually voting for a person who is going to have to give it their best judgment."

When constituents' views on an issue are divided, or when the views of a particular riding run counter to the prevailing interests or opinions across the country, an MP faces the thorny problem of which viewpoint to represent. As an MP, are you representing the people in your riding who voted for you? Are you representing *all* the people in your riding, including those who didn't vote for you? Are you representing people across the country? And how, in a modern, diverse society, is one to ascertain their views in any realistic way, or purport that their constituents share one view on any topic? "[It's a challenge] to find a balance," said Liberal MP Andy Mitchell. "You serve a national interest if you are sitting in Parliament, but you also serve local interests, which is the whole beauty in our system of having constituencies. You are accountable to the country as a whole, but also very specifically to the electors that put you in that office. [MPs] are driven by both those things."

This was particularly the case for MPs in Cabinet and party leadership positions, roles that forced them to adapt their initial conceptions of where an MP's focus should be. Some enjoyed the challenge in this, but for others leadership exacerbated the tensions already inherent in the role of an MP. "I believe to the core that the principal purpose of an MP is to represent [constituents]. . . . It was more difficult when I became the [party] leader because I occupied two roles simultaneously, one of which took you away from your constituents a lot," said Nova Scotian Alexa McDonough, a former NDP party leader.

For some leaders, this challenge was invigorating. "Part of your job is to try and build the threads that hold the country together," said former Liberal Cabinet minister and Edmonton MP Anne McLellan. "You've got to try and encourage people to be bigger than they think they can be in terms of spirit and vision."

Another group of more partisan MPs sidestepped the trustee/delegate dichotomy to emphasize a different primary purpose: representing to the rest of Parliament the views of one's political party. Some felt the party and the constituents were the primary groups to balance. "The purpose [of an MP] is to be a leader from your community in the national affairs of the country. On the one hand, you should be listening to the people you represent, and that means whoever is in the community and not just the people who voted for you," said former NDP leader Ed Broadbent. "[On the other hand], you've campaigned on your party's programs and issues and so you also have an obligation to that."

As Liberal MP Russ Powers told us (as cited in this book's introduction), his experience was that the party was at the centre of the MP's role: to develop policy that best serves the party, not necessarily the country. Like Powers, who spoke of the gap between the "canned thing of why . . . we're there" and "the truth," Jeremy Harrison, a Saskatchewan Conservative who served from 2004 to 2006, acknowledged the dominance of the party in how he did his job. "I think probably the primary thing that an MP can do right now, the way the system is developed, is to be kind of an ombudsman for your riding, and an advocate for your riding. That's kind of what most MPs would see as being their primary job . . . but I was much more political, I think, than your average political member," he said. "I was more involved in the party, more committed to the success of the leader. . . . I felt a real sense of, anything I could do to help Stephen [Harper] become PM I would do."

Others described the priorities of representation differently. Liberal MP Eleni Bakopanos portrayed the job as part of hierarchy that involved obligations to one's constituents, political party and party leader. Like many MPs, she recognized that she was elected under a political party banner, and owed some allegiance to that party. "[An MP's] first purpose is to serve the constituents," she said. "Second, whether you like it or not, you belong to a team. I think your loyalty to the values and principles of that political entity [are important]. Third, I think, is loyalty to the leader."

JUST AS Charles Hubbard remembers fondly helping his ailing former student navigate Service Canada, some MPs emphasized working in a service-oriented capacity for constituents not only as one of the job's most gratifying elements but as one of its primary purposes. "You're the ombudsman," explained Conservative MP Jim Gouk. "When there's a federal problem, you're the go-to guy. You're the one that they look to for help because if *you* can't help them, who can? You either help or put them in touch with someone who can. You listen to their problem." This can mean assisting constituents with the bureaucratic matters—immigration, employment insurance, passports or veterans' support. It also includes helping people benefit from federal programs or legislation, and fulfilling the role of a representative by attending social occasions or other commemorative events. In fact, about a quarter of the MPs we interviewed said this service to constituents, when they could operate freely from any party interference and the results were tangible and personal, was the best part of being an MP.

A few MPs, on the other hand, disagreed with what they saw as an over-demand for constituency service on the part of those they represented. Conservative MP for Prince Albert, Saskatchewan, Brian Fitzpatrick referred disparagingly to the "chamber of commerce" philosophy held by some mayors in his riding, which had them badgering him about what he was doing for the riding as its MP. Was he bringing them grant money that would create jobs? Was he wooing industry? "I guess I never really was strong on that area," Fitzpatrick said. "I didn't think that was the role. We're lawmakers—we're there to make sure that we pass good laws and so on. It's not like I'm a lobbyist, to bring industry and stuff to your riding. . . . It still bothers me, because philosophically I think the role of government is to create the proper environment so that enterprise and business operates in a free market, not with the government trying to give out grants and so on. So I always found it a bit distasteful to get involved with that stuff, but you're forced into it whether you like it or not."

Liberal MP Sue Barnes saw the importance of constituency work, but felt that most of it could—and should—be done by the staff at her local office. "I'm known for good constituency work, but I didn't do most of it—my staff did it on my behalf," she said. "I gave them the instructions, and they knew they'd be in trouble if they didn't do it." At the same time, she added, "To me [constituency work is] a sidebar." And she recognized that her constituents would have preferred she work directly on providing service in the riding. "It's something of a political truth that they don't care what you do somewhere else." However, Barnes saw the two as linked, and acknowledged that she chose her legislative priorities from among the issues that mattered to her constituents. She backed medical marijuana in 1999 and 2004, for example, because a constituent raised the issue with her. "A lot of things [were] sparked by individual constituent problems," Barnes said. "My interest in same-sex marriage came from a constituent who worked for me in my first campaign, and later died of AIDS—a very intelligent young man."

The late Reg Alcock, from Winnipeg South, approached his job in a similar way. "I had a riding in the south end. I had a railway running through it. The two railways are big in this town, less so now. Eight of the largest trucking firms are in this town. I had the University of Manitoba . . . in my riding. So what are the issues that I tend to take up? Transportation, post-secondary education. Not because anybody held a gun to my head, it's just that you try to serve the people who live there," he said.

Barnes takes the point further: "I think that generally people don't realize the skill set it takes to be an MP," she explained. "It's like running two businesses in two locations, managing supplies, staff, budgets, everything. I thought of my roles this way: In London, I'm dealing with the law as it now stands; in Ottawa the role was future-oriented: how things could be changed, how things could be improved. I divided my expertise that way."

REFLECTING AN ASPECT of the outsider's perspective we discussed earlier, some MPs described feeling an obligation to bring their own personal identities into Parliament. Liberal MP Paddy Torsney of Burlington, Ontario, elected less than a decade after she'd completed university, said that representing her demographic was an important aspect of her job as an MP. "[I have a responsibility] for broader representation and involvement with young people and women. . . . [I have] an obligation to speak up," she said. Montreal-area Liberal MP Eleni Bakopanos felt similarly. "I was the first Greek-born woman elected to the House of Commons," she said. "A lot of young women in the community [saw] me as a role model."

Similarly, many MPs expressed a desire to bring their personal version of the outsider narrative to Parliament. "My biggest concern was [giving] people an opportunity to be part of our society," said Liberal MP Charles Hubbard. And Paul Forseth, a Conservative originally elected in suburban Vancouver as a Reform MP, said, "I think there was a notion that somehow the average Canadian could take back Parliament and show that we can behave differently." Several MPs described wanting to change the way politics was conducted, or how politicians acted. Sue Barnes put it this way: "To me, the whole point of Parliament was to create change, to create good change. It wasn't to keep the status quo."

Gary Merasty particularly felt the burden of representing his Cree community in northern Saskatchewan. "They don't see you as a [party member], they see you as Gary, and

[say], 'Screw the political party affiliations, you better do what is good for our people.'" Marcel Lussier, a Brossard—La Prairie Bloc MP, described his job as representing Quebec internationally, and interacting with ambassadors of other countries. "Bloc MPs in Ottawa have a very big role to play at the international level. . . . I met over seventy ambassadors during my three years in Ottawa. . . . I am a representative of Quebec. . . . We are there to represent and express our ideas. And one of the events that I was very proud of was when Gilles Duceppe invited all of the ambassadors to meet with us, saying, 'I want to explain to foreign ambassadors the role and position of the Bloc concerning Quebec sovereignty.'"

Many of the MPs described their roles in language that did not fit neatly into any categories, using more colloquial descriptions that made little or no reference to conceptions of representation or to their political party. These descriptions included platitudes and personal observations, as well as statements that sought to embrace a wider sense of social good. "Your purpose is to advance the public interest, and that admittedly can be foggy to [define]," said Conservative MP Monte Solberg. "Ultimately, it boils down to working with your colleagues to advance the prosperity of people."

Another set regarded the role as a call to service. "Being an MP is not a job, it's a calling, a way of life. You are one of the lucky people to ever get there," said Liberal MP Roger Galloway. David Anderson, a fellow Liberal, lamented that the role was too often seen only as a stepping stone to Cabinet, rather than the opportunity for able people to contribute to the country.

The MPs were fond of comparing the job to other professions that often had little in common with an MP's job, except perhaps for a heavy interaction with people: professions such as administrator, doctor, priest, teacher, ambassador, social worker, messenger, spokesperson and lobbyist. Stéphane Bergeron, Bloc Québécois MP for Verchères, stressed his accountability function and equated the role to that of a "watchdog." Several likened the job to their own pre-parliamentary careers. Toronto-area Liberal MP Roy Cullen, an accountant and forestry executive, described the MP's role as akin to running a small business. "I used to say to my staff, you know, when a constituent comes in the door or calls, it's like our customer, right? You know, they're always right; I mean, they may not always be right, but they're always right. And so we've got to look after them, just like we'd look after a customer." Another, a lawyer and mediator, said the role was about encouraging collaboration among MPs to make things happen, regardless of party stripes. "The whole story of Parliament is human relationships at the level of the MP," said Liberal MP Paul Macklin. "We do that in our daily life in our communities: we build relationships; we build networks."

ALTOGETHER, THE EIGHTY MPs we interviewed used an astonishing variety of terms and concepts to describe the position. No doubt like many Canadians, we hadn't fully considered how MPs might define their roles, but we certainly expected greater agreement about why they were in Ottawa—and what they were there to do. If parliamentarians do not have a shared conception of an MP's job description, how are Canadians to know what MPs are supposed to be doing in office? And if citizens don't know what to expect from our elected officials, should we be surprised when they believe MPs don't deliver?

Bloc MP Stéphane Bergeron understood the role in terms that closely corresponded to the traditional Westminster definition of the MPs' position: "Collectively with colleagues, [an MP] must play a role as a watchdog of government activities, and ensure that the government [pursues] the public interests and spends money wisely." Surprisingly, only a few MPs described their jobs in terms that corresponded as much as Bergeron's with the Westminster standard: holding government accountable for its decisions and for the appropriate expenditure of tax dollars.

Some may argue that the wide variety in the MPs' descriptions of their role is inevitable. Contemporary Canadian society is culturally, regionally, economically and politically diverse, and much more so then when Canadian parliaments were first developed. "It's a question that will be answered, probably, in as many different ways as there are Members of Parliament and will probably change with the historic development of the country," former Kelowna-area Conservative MP Werner Schmidt observed. A further complication in Canada is that some MPs belong to political parties—such as the New Democratic Party or the Bloc Québécois—that historically have been unlikely to win enough seats to form a government. These MPs expect to be members of the opposition benches, and that expectation undoubtedly influences their interpretation of an MP's essential purpose.

Even still, the huge range of views was troubling. Surely we can do better than the current inconsistent, and even contradictory, understanding of what an MP is supposed to do. As reported in the previous chapter, MPs told us they received almost no orientation or training, and were forced to devise their own means of preparing for the job. So, we have an unprepared and unsupported new contingent of Parliament whose members, freshly arrived or seasoned, display fundamental differences of opinion on the basic aspects of their job, and what they were elected to do.

This disparity creates several identifiable problems. First, a lack of clarity about a job description makes it more difficult to do that job. This is particularly the case when MPs must navigate the tensions among their own preferences, those of their constituents, their party platform and leaders' priorities. A lack of clarity in one's job description means that critical tasks will be overlooked. Efforts will be duplicated. Important work will be neglected, or left incomplete. In any large undertaking that requires the participation of many different people, roles and responsibilities need to be clearly defined. And governing Canada qualifies as a large undertaking. With a high degree of uncertainty about who is responsible to whom and for what, interpersonal tension is bound to arise. And such tensions tend to be amplified in times of conflict or uncertainty—times that especially demand clear-headed, well-reasoned responses from our elected leaders.

An additional problem is that this confusion among role definitions makes it difficult for the media who observe Parliament to report to Canadians how effectively the country is being governed. Organizations that operate without a shared sense of purpose or responsibility are more difficult to understand, explain and assess, and can create a lot of noise that causes people to turn away. As a corollary, whether through impressions formed by media coverage or through direct interaction with politicians, this lack of clarity about what MPs are supposed to be doing is conveyed to the electorate, and can confuse voters. At the same time, if MPs themselves are unable to describe their own roles clearly and coherently, it is hard to blame the media or the public for not understanding the roles either.

Of course, with MPs' divergent priorities and differing levels of power, it cannot be expected that every MP will do the job in exactly the same way. A system like ours, with little orientation or training, without any agreed-upon job description, in fact requires that new MPs find their own way. As so many MPs described it to us, they arrived in Ottawa and were forced to make do, to play a form of political "fake it 'til you make it." The beneficial side to this is that it leaves a wide latitude for MPs to pursue their own or their constituents' objectives—a strength of the system that can allow enterprising, entrepreneurial MPs to bring forward new ideas.

That said, the input of multiple interests can also cause, and most certainly exacerbate confusion, partisanship and a blinkered focus on the short term and, in particular, on the next election. Without an agreed-upon sense of purpose, an evaluation of success will be equally unclear and difficult to accomplish. What is the simplest and most immediate indication of politicians' success? Getting re-elected. As far as indicators of parliamentarians' success go in public life, being given another crack at the job is hardly satisfactory.

BUT HOW DOES A person actually excel at the job? How does a new MP get ahead? When asked to proffer advice to their incoming colleagues, by far the most common imperative suggested by our interviewed former Members of Parliament was: become an expert in something. Ideally, the advice went, that expertise is shared by few other colleagues and by no bigwigs in the party; nor is it necessarily something they care about. That apathy from above allows you to become the go-to figure in your party. Learn everything you can about that topic, and then identify what you can do to improve it. If, as some of our MPs have suggested, politicians exhibit a pack mentality, this advice would boil down to the following: Find your own bone, and chew on that.

Such "freelancing"—beginning with sniffing out a needed area of expertise that is of interest—requires an entrepreneur's creativity and initiative. And drive and discipline are needed for poring over policy briefs and the minutiae of the legislative history in such areas as Canada's food regulations, immigration policies or bankruptcy law.

Former prime minister Paul Martin honed the description the freelancing imperative: "For God's sake, develop a couple of areas [of expertise]," he said. "Don't develop fifty. . . . Don't just pick an area that everybody is doing. Think of some of the areas in which you could really be called on . . . if that happens then the odds are better that you're going to get into Cabinet. But even if [that doesn't happen], then you establish yourself as a parliamentarian of great worth."

Calling this imperative "advice" is perhaps putting it too mildly. Our MPs didn't just suggest it. They said: You *have* to freelance. Unless you are a member of the inner circle, say, a Cabinet member who has the PM's ear, or on an important committee, then your opinion doesn't much affect major legislation. So, if you want to make a difference, if you want to feel as though you are adding value to Parliament, if you want to actually see your fingerprints on something that improves

Canada, then you have to go off and find something that hasn't yet entered the radar field of the leadership.

Sometimes an MP of lesser stature can make great change that way. One of the most illustrative stories about freelancing that we heard involved David Anderson, the former Liberal minister of the environment, who was elected for the first time in the B.C. riding of Esquimalt–Saanich at the age of thirty-one, eight years after he'd won a silver medal in rowing in the 1960 Rome Summer Games.

In the late '60s Anderson was developing one of these outlying specialties in a topic about which few of his fellow federal politicians cared: oil transport, specifically tanker safety and pipeline failsafe mechanisms. Through his work on increasing the safety of transporting that natural resource, he had been frustrated by the fact that a given issue could require him to approach the natural resources committee, or perhaps the fisheries committee, or sometimes the agriculture committee. Anderson proposed a new single committee that would focus exclusively on environmental matters. But the nascent environmental movement had yet to gain any traction in political circles, and his senior colleagues in the Liberal Party disagreed—particularly Government House Leader Donald Macdonald, who wished to decrease the number of committees on the Hill.

Anderson pressed on. He began studying the rules of the House, and he realized that he might, if he caught a few breaks, be able to do something that would sneak an environmental committee into existence. "You know," he recalls, "there are very, very, very few MPs who know anything about the rules of the House . . . but if anyone wants to quickly get extra chips for the poker game they're playing, learning the rules is the fastest way of getting yourself in a very good position."

According to Anderson's account, the execution of his plan began during his attendance in the legislature on House Duty on a Friday afternoon, when only a few dozen MPs were present. Anderson submitted a motion to create the Special Committee on Environmental Pollution, which provided him with the chance to address the rest of the House. Only the chance, however. Anderson's name was put into a hat along with the names of other MPs who had introduced motions. He'd been selected and allocated time for his matter to be discussed in the House. Normally that was a snoozefest. The MP who had introduced the motion stood up, gave a spiel, and then an opposition MP would get up and respond, after which the time was up and the Speaker would say, "Well, we'll take this up in the next session of the House." By the next session, everyone had usually lost interest. Or the inconvenience of going through the process again, from the start, usually acted to dissuade another attempt.

But Anderson had something unconventional up his sleeve. The next part of the plan involved a fine point he had learned from studying the rules—something he'd earlier buttonholed the Speaker about, just to clarify that Anderson's understanding of the rules was correct. "You can do that?" Anderson said to the Speaker, Lucien Lamoureux, a one-time Liberal MP who'd successfully run in Stormont–Dundas as an Independent in the '68 election that had also brought Anderson to the Hill. "It's *really* like that?" And Lamoureux confirmed that it was—an archaic little convention left over from Parliament's early days.

On the Friday when he was lucky enough for his turn to come up, David Anderson simply nodded at the Speaker. And the Speaker recognized Anderson, meaning the bill proceeded to the floor. All told, there were only about thirty people in the House. And no one was paying any attention to the young backbench MP. They were writing letters. They were talking to each other. Maybe there was an MP here or there besides the Speaker who noticed. But the unusual thing was, Anderson didn't get up to speak. Nobody else got up to speak, either, because they expected Anderson to be the first. But Anderson didn't move. He just sat there. The Speaker waited, and waited, and then he did what the rules required him to do if a motion went to the floor and no one stood up to speak. *The Speaker called the vote.* He asked the MPs to decide on Anderson's legislation. This was the final part of Anderson's plan. The young MP knew that no one was really paying attention—no one expected anything of importance to come up at such a sparsely attended House on a Friday. "So everybody heard, 'all in favour,' and they all said 'aye,' thinking this was the vote to put my motion on the floor to be discussed. It wasn't. It was a motion at that point—my motion. They passed it by accident."

So the Special Committee on Environmental Pollution was born—much to the annoyance of Donald Macdonald. "He made reference to the fact that I needed a good walk across the Ottawa River in cement shoes," Anderson recalled. "It was a good example of [how] a little knowledge of the rules meant a lot."

HOW DOES FREELANCING begin? Usually by chance, and as a response to circumstances in an MP's riding. That's what happened with Conservative MP Randy White's work in the penal system. "In Fraser Valley there are seven prisons," White said. "There's lots of crime there. It seemed like every third, fourth or fifth person came through my door with a terrible story about being a victim. So the more I worked on that the more I got involved in it. . . . Anywhere that victims needed help, normally I would show up if I could." I became such an expert in issues related to crime and the penal system, he continued, "that when I stood up in the House of Commons and said something, people would say, 'Don't challenge this guy. He knows what he's talking about.'"

In another example, Bloc Québécois MP Roger Clavet encountered a problem involving a foreign student who lived in Clavet's riding of Louis-Hébert. The man was from the African country of Togo and was studying at Laval University. He was frustrated by labour regulations that prevented him from working anywhere but at an on-campus business at a time when the local Chamber of Commerce wanted to hire graduate students. The student appealed to Clavet for help, and Clavet in turn appealed to Minister of Citizenship and Immigration Joe Volpe, a Liberal—but nothing could be done in time. Clavet had to break it to the Togolese student that he couldn't work, and the man left the country. But Clavet kept at it. He developed an expertise in this aspect of immigration law, and worked with Volpe until the minister took steps to change the regulations to allow foreign students to work off-campus while pursuing their studies.

Conservative MP Jim Gouk freelanced for a change in the rules regarding Employment Insurance after a furniture factory went bankrupt in one of his constituency's towns in the south

Okanagan. "The workers thought, 'Oh my God, you know, all of a sudden we're out of a job and all we're going to have is EI,'" Gouk said, recounting the story. But then the workers discovered they weren't even entitled to EI. The problem? They were entitled to severance pay—and according to the regulations, anyone due severance pay couldn't get EI. Never mind that they weren't going to get any severance pay in any case, because the furniture factory was bankrupt. But the rules were blind to the difference. "The rules as they read at the time were that if you were entitled to severance pay, then you don't get EI until you've used up severance—you're entitled to six weeks' severance and you can't apply for EI until the six weeks are up and then you've got a waiting period," Gouk explained. So Gouk got on the phone. He sat down with the minister responsible and told him the problem and, according to Gouk, the minister was astonished. Gouk's work obtained EI money for the factory employees, but more significantly, he also successfully pushed to have the rule changed, so that similarly out-of-work labourers wouldn't face the same situation.

All of this is great work, on the face of it. However, something about the freelancing imperative seems like a symptom of a deeper problem: the struggle of backbench MPs to find an active role in the governing of the country by being involved in crafting policy proposals or major pieces of legislation. Interpreted one way, the act of freelancing is a surrender. Conceding any role in the things the party cares about, the freelancing MP heads off to find an area *no one* in Parliament cares about, and vows to make a mark there. The positive spin lauds the entrepreneurial spirit that freelancing requires, and enables MPs like David Anderson, when the winds blow in the right direction, to tilt the sails, lean in and be part of creating national change. But we wonder whether the imperative to freelance would be more accurately described as pushing MPs' work into the realm of mere chance.

WHEN WE ASKED former MPs to identify their greatest achievements in office, freelancing played significantly into their responses. We noticed that few mentioned things that happened because they held power, or because they had a hand in the government agenda. Perhaps echoing their earlier outsider sentiment, they were most proud of the things they'd achieved by working entrepreneurially, outside the traditional lines of power.

Given the centrality of the political party to the MPs' existence, we'd expected that a few of our interview subjects might have mentioned their successes in furthering their parties' priorities for the country. But very few mentioned being a good party soldier, or anything remotely related. Through the very stories they chose to highlight, they again tried to tell us that they weren't politicians like Canadians expect politicians to be. They were not among those partisan operatives we see on TV, hollering in Question Period, their concerns far removed from the daily realities of most Canadians. That was someone else. *They* were different.

MPs' proudest moments often involved bringing a constituency's concerns to the federal level, like Randy White's work on victims' rights. Or they'd include stories of cooperation with fellow MPs or with political opponents, like Roger Clavet's work with the Liberal minister on immigration reform. Or their successes involved helping constituents navigate federal bureaucracies, which occasionally led to legislative changes—as happened with Jim Gouk and the EI regulations. But such cases of advocacy leading to legislative change were exceptional.

Take Paul Forseth's advocacy for an African refugee struggling with an immigration problem. The man had been accepted into Canada as a political refugee, but then faced difficulties with Immigration when he applied to bring over his wife and children. Citizenship and Immigration Canada didn't recognize the marriage because the couple didn't have the proper documentation—they couldn't produce a marriage certificate. "The government said, 'No, you don't have a wife. You are just committing a fraud. These kids aren't really your kids because you can't provide the documentary evidence,'" Forseth explained.

The Canadian government required this man to pay for DNA testing to establish his paternity. "All of his original story was eventually proven true," Forseth said. But by the time Forseth had helped the man sort it all out and bring his family to Canada, the man hadn't seen his wife and children for seven years. "They came into my office to say thank you, and they dressed up in their national costumes and we took a picture together," recalled Forseth. "That was quite a proud moment—being able to help him deal with the bureaucracy and the thousands of dollars that he spent trying to phone and speak to his wife. . . . All of the various stages that we went through to reunite that family after all they had been through, and to welcome them to Canada, and I had a small part in bringing that family together—that was pretty emotional. So, that was a good one."

It's a noble pursuit, helping frustrated citizens deal with the federal government's most difficult bureaucracies, whether with passport applications, immigration claims or pension problems. But the practice raises a larger question: Should our Members of Parliament really be spending their time on such issues? The traditional definition of an MP in the Westminster system of government—to consider, refine and pass legislation, and to hold the government to account—suggests not. Eleni Bakopanos, for one, agreed: "That was the hard part," she said, "trying to explain to somebody, especially immigration cases, where we were limited in how far we could intervene. . . . It should not be the MP's office handling that."

Bakopanos is right. The practice of MPs intervening in immigration, employment insurance, veterans' affairs, Canada pension and disability cases raises difficult questions about political interference in a process that is meant to be handled by an objective bureaucracy. Judging from the MPs' reports of their efforts, Canadians, and would-be Canadians, are receiving unequal and inconsistent treatment. If you know an MP, or if an MP takes an interest in your case, then it seems likely you'll get better service. Is the Canadian federal bureaucracy one that functions better on the basis of who you know? Do citizens who happen to be Conservative Party members receive the same level of service from their MPs in Liberal-held ridings? What about NDP, Green or Bloc party members? It is a precept of our democratic government that our party affiliation should not act as an advantage, or disadvantage, in our dealings with bureaucrats.

Party affiliation aside, one's ability to solicit help from an MP can also be enhanced by a personal connection. In other countries where politicians interact with government in such a manner, those activities are referred to as corruption. Ideally, our bureaucracy should be equally accessible for all, regardless of whether one happened to catch the MP's attention, or helped out in a certain political campaign.

Then there's the question of appropriate focus. Working for their constituents in this way, our MPs are acting as de facto front-line service representatives for the federal government. Should an MP's job description include the imperative to paper over a broken bureaucracy? Or should the federal bureaucracy's decision-making processes be made more transparent and accessible to citizens, so that the burden of this work can be taken out of MPs' offices and placed back in the bureaucrats' hands, where it belongs?

Another question the practice poses: Is it the most effective use of our parliamentarians' time? Many Members of Parliament are spending valuable time and energy acting as intermediaries between individuals and the federal government. But rather than responding to citizen complaints about, say, an immigration process gone awry, rather than untangling the individual snarls symptomatic of a flawed system, shouldn't MPs more productively devote their energies toward reforming these snarled bureaucracies? Toward streamlining our nation's immigration application processes? To improving the customer service provided by Revenue Canada and perhaps simplifying the tax code? To fixing the approvals processes of the pension and employment insurance systems?

All that said, it takes only a little analysis to understand what's motivating the phenomenon, at least from the MPs' perspective. Part of it might be decent human kindness: after all, people can arrive at an MP's office in pretty dire straits, and it is human nature to want to assist. It also helps MPs take the pulse of the people they represented. "The constituency work is the reality check," said John Godfrey in an interview on CBC Radio's *The Current* about his exit interview. "You can be far too abstract if you're not dealing with real people, one at a time, sitting in front of you, with real problems."

Let's not fool ourselves, here, however: a constituent assisted by an MP is a constituent who is likely to vote for that MP in the next election. More fundamentally, constituent service is a manifestation of the same factors that encourage and perpetuate MP freelancing. In many ways, this customer service work is the logical extreme of freelancing. Helping constituents to fill out paperwork, immigration forms, passport advocacy—this is what our federal political representatives descend to when our political system renders them impotent. It's a logical symptom of the MPs' absence of power.

An MP typically starts out as a backbencher who isn't allowed much control over her political career. She doesn't choose the committee on which she serves. Her press releases, and increasingly her parliamentary speaking points, are pre-written and approved by the leader's office. And she certainly doesn't get much input on the important aspects of government legislation. So how does she assert herself? How does she work in a manner that gives her personal satisfaction and the feeling that she's made the most of her time in office? Acting as a customer service rep for the federal government is perhaps the easiest way to do that. This is labour that the MPs can control.

It wasn't always this way. Don Boudria, the Liberal MP from Glengarry–Prescott–Russell who is legendary for his enthusiasm for constituency work, described the way the MP has evolved into "a personal ombudsman for the grievances of electors." In fact, he regards this role as so entrenched in the job of the MP that he considers it an additional component to the job description.

"That is to say," Boudria explained, "Mrs. Smith goes to see you because she's been disqualified from EI. Why can she not get EI? . . . Well, as it ended up when the lead guy from EI contacted her to see if she was available, they have disconnected her phone because she had no money to pay [for] it, and there are all sorts of extenuating circumstances—and the MP is supposed to sort through that, and defend the grievances of their constituents. Whether it's my hypothetical EI case here, or the mother-in-law who lives in Lebanon who couldn't come to her grandchild's wedding because some immigration official goofed—or some other situation like that. And they happen like that every single day."

Boudria acknowledges that this situation isn't ideal. "To me," he says, "it talks a lot about faults in the system if the system is designed in such a way that MPs have become an appellate court for the entire bureaucracy—then there is something wrong with that part of the bureaucracy, or the structure under which they work." Nevertheless, fatalistically, he accepts it.

Not so his parliamentary colleague Bill Blaikie of the NDP. In federal political office from 1979 to 2008 and thus the longest-serving MP we interviewed, Blaikie worries that MPs' direct work with individual constituents, whether it involves attending someone's birthday celebration or helping with a component of the Ottawa bureaucracy, becomes "a kind of a substitute for real political input and real political activity." He wonders whether this "just naturally happens when people are further and further away from power . . . to give meaning to your life as an MP." And to establish the point, he brings up one of his legislative heroes, an MP named James Shaver Woodsworth, the founding leader of the CCF, who served in Parliament for the seventeen years from 1925 to 1942. Woodsworth, Blaikie says, focused on representing the whole of his constituency rather than on his relations with individual constituents—something Blaikie also tried to do. When asked by a constituent to do something that fell into an ombudsman or direct service role, Blaikie would say, "No—no, I can't do that. I am in Ottawa. I am doing the job you elected me to do."

Freelancing can result in some wonderful legislative work—such as David Anderson's stickhandling into existence the Canadian Parliament's first environment committee, or Jim Gouk advocating for changes to Employment Insurance. But too often it results in MPs resorting to acting as ombudsmen for the federal bureaucracy in order to feel as though they were making a difference.

With that in mind, it's time to consider giving our MPs a proper job description. It is a critical job in our democracy, and there needs to be some consistency in our collective understanding of its key components, responsibilities and expectations. Let's begin with their responsibilities in Ottawa. If MPs aren't given a clear sense of what's expected of them on the job, who's really to blame when that job doesn't get done?

CHAPTER FIVE

Kindergarten on the Rideau

The House of Commons is the venue where MPs gather for one of the most important aspects of their job—discussing the governance of our country. The House, first opened in 1920 after a fire destroyed the previous building, forms an impressive architectural space in the Centre Block of Canada's Houses of Parliament. The Chamber is dominated by Gothic Revival stone archways, stained glass and carved wood, and lit by majestic chandeliers. The ornately carved chair belonging to the Speaker, the presiding officer of the Commons, anchors the room. To the Speaker's right are the seats usually designated for the party that forms the government. The prime minister sits in the middle of the first aisle, with the Cabinet in the front rows. On the other side of the House, appropriately, the opposition side, the remaining seats accommodate the non-governing opposition parties— and sometimes, if the government holds a large majority, some backbench government MPs as well.

Canada's legislative assembly serves many functions. Foremost is its role as the public forum for debating the bene- fits and disadvantages of legislation, and for the passage or dissolution of that legislation. In addition, through Members' Statements, MPs have the opportunity to recognize the service of various Canadians and events of local significance in Parliament's official record, Hansard. MPs in the House of Commons can register petitions. And the most observed part of the House is Question Period, the forty-five-minute daily session that allows MPs to pose questions to and gather information from the government.

That, at least, is what is *supposed* to happen in the House. But our interviews reflect that little substantive policy discussion actually does take place in those hallowed chambers. The debate that leads to productive legislative change more often happens in places that are less public and where MPs can speak to one another more frankly, such as in committees or in caucus.

In practice, the parties use the House for other functions. What stands out for anyone who watches the proceedings is the sniping and quibbling that occurs among the MPs of various parties. In addition to its nominal function as a legislative assembly, the House, and more specifically, Question Period, is usurped as a grand venue for MPs to insult one another, to attack one another's platforms and to belittle opponents' achievements—to score points against one another in front of the press. It's where they engage in a form of extremely partisan, and, considering all the costs incurred to keep the House running, extremely expensive, form of political marketing.

Each party devotes considerable resources to orchestrating its MPs' behaviour in the House of Commons. The House Leader, for example, oversees the journey of a bill into law, as well as the rehearsal of and responses to questions expected to come from the opposition during Question Period. An Opposition House Leader does much the same thing but from their point of view. Ranking slightly below the House Leaders are the whips, who make sure their party's MPs show up and vote on tabled legislation according to the party's preferences. Whips are MPs who also serve polling functions that see them act as conduits to the leader for MPs' concerns about their party's positions. Finally, the whip has a role in scheduling and the assignment of party MPs to various committees. The whip also has enormous influence in deciding which members speak during proceedings in the House of Commons, including Question Periods and Members' Statements.

Few people in the country are more familiar with the way parties make use of their whips in the House of Commons than former Conservative MP for Prince George–Peace River Jay Hill. During his seventeen years as a Member of Parliament, Hill was chief whip for the Reform Party, the Canadian Alliance and the Conservative Party of Canada, and he served that function both in government and in opposition. He was also his party's House Leader in government and in opposition, and served twice as his party's Question Period director, specifically responsible for orchestrating which questions are asked, and by whom. "I don't think there was any MP from any party who was more involved in the day-to-day tactics and strategy of the House, of the Chamber, than I was," said Hill, speaking of his last decade in the House of Commons, from 2000 until 2010.

Hill was blunt and refreshingly open when discussing the House of Commons with us. His was the story of a remarkable evolution—one of the most senior figures in his party, who would come to sour on the tactics that parties employed in the House.

Hill did work to reduce the level of partisanship that the Conservatives employed. When he started work as Government House Leader after the October 2008 election, he realized there was an opportunity for a change from the practice of his predecessor, a man renowned for the opprobrium, über-partisanship and rhetorical flourishes he employed to criticize the opposition. In fact, when Prime Minister Stephen Harper asked Hill to become Government House Leader, Hill told the prime minister that he wouldn't operate the way his prede-cessor had. "I am just not going to," Hill recalls saying. "Sure, if it's a partisan attack, answer in a partisan way—but if it is a legitimate question about defence spending or whatever, stand up and give them an answer.

"Look, I will try and do the job," Hill reported telling the prime minister. It was the start of the Conservatives' second minority government, so the stakes were high. "I am going to try and get some legislation, get something accomplished, not only for our government but for our country—but having said that, if I am going to be negotiating in some cases on a minute-by-minute, or certainly hour-by-hour, basis with the opposi-tion parties to try and accomplish something, I can't then for forty-five minutes of the day get up and deliver partisan attacks on them, and then half an hour later be sitting down with them trying to say, how can we work through this and actually accomplish something?"

Soon after Hill became House Leader, he noticed MPs increasingly used their Members' Statements to issue "extremely partisan personal attacks that really poisoned the atmosphere of the Chamber." Hill referred to these attacks, particularly targeted toward Liberal leader Michael Ignatieff, as "partisan drivel," and he became very uneasy about them. Time and again, in Members' Statements, Conservative MPs would stand up and deliver withering sixty-second tirades against the Liberal leader, the exclusive purpose of which seemed to be to denigrate his character.

"Mr. Speaker," began one classic example from the Conservative MP from Peace River, Chris Warkentin, on May 29, 2009, in the wake of Ignatieff's criticizing the Conservatives for using without permission a nine-second C-SPAN clip of the Liberal leader. "The Liberal leader seems to be a fan of cover-ups. Perhaps he is just paranoid. The Liberal Party of Canada had its legions of lawyers attempt to stop the use of a video clip that its leader had during the time that he spent on C-SPAN . . . Clearly, the Liberals are trying to hide their leader's statements when he called America his country. Is that because the only thing he missed while he was outside of our country was Algonquin Park?"

Soon after Warkentin's invective came another broadside, this one by the MP for Beauport–Limoilou in Quebec, Sylvie Boucher: "Mr. Speaker, in recent days, we have watched as the Liberals have ramped up the worst sort of political partisanship. . . . This pernicious partisanship clearly shows that the policies of the Liberal Party are devoid of ideas and lack direction."

Next up was Tom Lukiwski, MP for Regina–Lumsden–Lake Centre: "Mr. Speaker," Lukiwski said. "Liberal hypocrisy is at an all-time high. On one hand, the Liberals are attacking the size of the deficit and, on the other hand, they are demanding billions more in spending." And soon after: "Mr. Speaker, when things do not go their way, the Liberals go running for cover," said Saint Boniface MP Shelly Glover. "In fact, hypocrisy is at an all-time high with the Liberal Party."

What made these partisan jabs all the more remarkable was their setting. Members' Statements were more traditionally used by members for *nice* things. The day's first statement, for example, featured Conservative Brent Rathgeber recognizing the volunteers who donated their time to help run the twenty-eighth annual International Children's Festival in St. Albert. Liberal Keith Martin spoke about the Roots and Shoots program founded by primatologist Dr. Jane Goodall, which encouraged children to help the environment. And the Bloc's Nicolas Dufour recognized the Quebec country music legend Roger Miron, celebrating his eightieth birthday that week.

So Hill's reluctance to allow this practice—also perpetuated by parties other than his own—was understandable, even if he wasn't always able to contain it. "It really got over the top, way over the top. I was very uncomfortable with it," Hill said. Many caucus members came to him to complain that things were getting out of hand. In response, Hill told his colleagues: "The only way we will ever get that to stop is [if] enough of you refuse. It's *your* Members' Statement. You are an individual Member of Parliament. I understand that the staff phones you, and they lean on you, and you understand it's coming right from the boss, but if you refuse to stand in your place and deliver that statement—and some did, to their credit, quite a number did—but they would always find people who wanted to be up on television."

———

IT HAS BEEN OBSERVED before that the House of Commons public visitors' gallery attracts schoolchildren from all over the country. These students come expecting to see our nation's leaders debating the issues of the day with dignity and decorum, only to find these elected men and women conducting themselves like kids at the back of the school bus. (The precise number of teachers who bring their students from the far reaches of Canada to sit in the Commons visitors' gallery is unknown, but many MPs mention the visits as a way to illustrate their disgust.) Across all our interviews, MPs claimed to be embarrassed by the public displays of acrimony and repeatedly stressed that these displays misrepresent how politics actually operates.

Again, MPs professed to be different from the typical politicians seen on TV. They worried whether the insulting rhetoric—perpetuated by their colleagues, they insisted—contributes to a growing sense of political disaffection among Canadians, hypothesizing that it causes viewing audiences to get turned off by politics. The conduct on display in the House is indeed beneath our MPs; and whereas vigorous, considered debate is welcome, partisan attacks and feigned outrage discourage people from paying attention, let alone engaging in politics. Party leaders and their professional staffs devote a lot of resources to engineering the histrionics of the House. These behaviours distract MPs from engaging in substantive policy debates—which may just suit the party leaders' purposes. Perhaps MPs who think they are helping their party by point-scoring and insulting are less likely to realize how little they're contributing to legislative policy.

"I found it quite difficult sometimes," said NDP MP Catherine Bell. "The decorum in the House—there should be stricter rules and the Speaker should be held to account because he has the last say. . . . When you stand up to make your statement, which is your right, and there are people yelling at you, it's nasty. To me, it's mean. . . . I have seen kindergartners act better. . . . What bothers me is that every day in Question Period, the gallery fills up with schoolchildren and that is what they see. They don't see people debating in committees—they see people yelling at each other."

The partisanship is overplayed, anyway, the MPs said. Several attributed it to an exaggeration of small differences intended by the professional political staff who work in the prime minister's and opposition leaders' offices to distinguish the parties and what they stand for, and to fire up their partisan bases (how many of these partisans are really listening, however, is perhaps a more important consideration). "The debate between the Liberals and the Conservatives on income tax is not whether there should be *no* income taxes, or 100 percent income taxes, it's whether the rate should be 29 percent at the high end versus 25," said Monte Solberg. "You know, the debate really is not very big at all, so it's really quite disingenuous to characterize the other side as being bad or evil. It's crazy to talk that way. . . . When the government's way off base and you think it will affect a fundamental right, by all means go after them hard and make them pay the price. [But] most of the time, it's not that. It's degrees of difference."

What needs to change in order to enhance the representative work of MPs and their parties on Parliament Hill so as to make it relevant to Canadians?

Let's start where we just were—with Question Period itself. Tuning in to political news in Canada often means watching, listening to or reading about these forty-five minutes a day. Intended as a forum for the opposition to hold the government to account by asking questions of its representatives, Question Period takes place every weekday that Parliament is in session, at 2:15 every afternoon except Friday, when it's held at 11:15 in the morning. Since 1977 the proceedings have been televised and today CPAC, the parliamentary channel jointly owned by a consortium of Canadian cable broadcasters, airs the sessions live. All this makes Question Period the most publicized aspect of Parliament. And why not? With all the heckling and carrying on, it makes for great TV. It also serves to reinforce Canadians' sense that MPs are wasting time in Ottawa. "The unfortunate thing is that Question Period is used as the barometer of what goes on in Ottawa," said Liberal MP Roy Cullen. "It is really a zoo. It's theatre."

Liberal-turned-Green MP Blair Wilson recalled giving a disclaimer to tourists visiting from his constituency in British Columbia. "They'd come to Question Period and I would say the same speech every time. 'What you are about to see is not what I do on a daily basis. This is forty-five minutes of entertainment on television. This is just to feed the [media] jackals. . . . These are kids in a sandbox.'

"I am embarrassed by it," Wilson said. "It's all about the sound bites. The success of Question Period is based upon, 'Did you get your twenty seconds on the eleven o'clock news?' . . . So, even though this is what everybody sees, this is not what government is all about."

Wilson spoke highly of his fellow MPs' intentions. They were in Ottawa with similar goals of making Canada the best place in the world to live. "We have got to figure out the systems you need to put in place that will achieve those goals," Wilson said. "Question Period does not achieve those goals."

Our interviewed MPs also professed to dislike how the party leadership and staff "staged" Question Period. Here we see a difference from the British Parliament, which doesn't actually have enough seats in its legislative chamber to accommodate all of Britain's 650 MPs—an intentional choice that reflects the reality that not all MPs choose to be in the Chamber at the same time. On TV, the British Parliament's smaller capacity makes the place look crowded with only a fraction of its complete assembly. Canada's House of Commons is different—although currently it has only about half the number of Britain's MPs, our House is designed to accommodate all the MPs simultaneously, each with his or her own desk. So, making it appear crowded during parliamentary debate requires a fair bit of seat-switching. Bloc MP Odina Desrochers characterized MPs in Question Period as "potted plants," moved around for decoration, because leaders and whips want their MPs present in Parliament to gather around an MP asking a question—to ensure that the proceedings look more vibrant for television and to give the appearance that MPs had all shown up for work to support their leader. However, the staging also made some MPs feel less than essential to their party's effectiveness in Parliament. "If all you do is show up at Question Period and clap when it's necessary, you can get pretty frustrated," said Russ Powers, the Liberal MP. Colleen Beaumier, another Liberal, echoed the complaint: "How much time did I need to stand there and clap like a trained seal?"

There's a perception among some MPs, the media and the population at large that Question Period represents the most problematic aspect of Ottawa. "Question Period isn't the root of what ails our politics," wrote Paul Wells in a *Maclean's* column that neatly sums up this sentiment. "But it is most certainly the hub, the swamp, the KICK ME HERE sign where everything we hate converges every day. The half-truths, the confected fury, the mayfly attention span, the ritual humiliation of the thoughtful or eccentric. And above all, the waste: of time, energy, hope.

"Question Period is broken," Wells concludes. "It poisons the rest of the day and our democracy with it. We're not protecting accountability by preserving this charade. We're mocking it."

Most of the MPs we consulted were of the same opinion. In fact, so many criticized Question Period and distanced themselves from what happens there that we found it disingenuous—it seems likely that the very same MPs who criticized Question Period had, at one time or another, participated in the personal attacks and desk-thumping theatrics that ultimately strain the public's perception of our politics and those who practise it.

We should acknowledge that some MPs lauded Question Period's role in holding the government to account; the fact that most of the positive depictions of Question Period came from Liberals may involve the timing of our interviews, which occurred just after the Liberals had lost power and had switched to functioning as the Official Opposition. "It's important to democracy," said former Thunder Bay–Rainy River Liberal MP Ken Boshcoff. "Of course it produces acting and grandstanding, but it also produces accountability."

"I love the forum of Question Period," said former Liberal MP Omar Alghabra. "I know there is heckling and all that stuff, but I really think that is superficial. Just imagine, it's the only democracy in the world where the executive comes to a session not knowing what questions they are going to be asked. They are being asked in public, so it is quite a vital and important instrument in our democracy—I like Question Period and the role that it serves."

"Most people think Question Period is just a big circus with a bunch of idiots screaming at one another," said Liberal MP Bill Graham. "I was a participant in Question Period. I loved it. It was great fun. I preferred it when I was the minister answering [rather] than when I was the leader having to ask. . . . I say with pride that we have one of the few parliamentary democracies left in the world where the prime minister is in the House two or three days a week for Question Period. The British prime minister comes once a month. . . . The Canadian system is still the one where the prime minister is personally standing there and I think that is a wonderful thing."

A few Conservatives admitted having fun in Question Period as well. "I liked Question Period," said Jeremy Harrison. "When you could get up, and you knew you delivered a good question and you knew you scored some points. That was a good feeling. I enjoyed that."

THE HOUSE OF COMMONS is more than just the hour a day devoted to Question Period and Members' Statements. In fact, only about 10 percent of the words spoken in the House are uttered during Question Period, which comprises only forty-five minutes of what's typically a seven-hour day. About 60 percent of the House's time is spent in Government Business, where the agenda is set largely by the government. During this time, bills proposed by ministers are debated, and the budget and supporting estimates that outline the government's expenditures are put forward for parliamentary approval. The major exceptions are the twenty-two days each year in which the government must allow the opposition to determine the topic of debate.

An hour each day is dedicated to debating bills and motions proposed by individual MPs who are not parliamentary secretaries or in Cabinet. Typically, one proposal is debated during the one-hour period. (The order is established at the very beginning of a session by a random draw among MPs' names, meaning not all proposals will be debated.) Another category of business in the House is known as Routine Proceedings, which provide members and ministers with an opportunity to bring a variety of matters to the attention of the House, including citizen petitions and House Committee reports. The amount of time allotted to Routine Proceedings varies from day to day according to the agenda.

Most Canadians don't witness the full range of this debate, and frankly neither do most MPs. Apart from Question Period, most are present only when they're on House Duty—a few hours each week assigned by their whips when MPs are required to attend debates in the House and represent their party's positions. Given the overall poor attendance, and the fact that the parties and the media focus nearly all their attention on Question Period, most MPs we spoke to viewed House Duty as monotonous and generally a waste of time.

"Outside of Question Period, it was dead in the House," said Jeremy Harrison, capturing the sentiment of many of his colleagues. "There were twenty to thirty people there. They're on their computer, catching up on correspondence. They're there because they have to be. There are very few members who are there because they want to be."

"You don't attend the House except for your [assigned] duty day," said Liberal MP David Anderson. "So a speech is made to a House of twenty, maybe forty, people. The media do not report them, or if they report anything, they report from the written records."

MPs or their leaders did little to alter this state of affairs. For example, several MPs said they were told to make speeches on subjects they knew nothing about. One newly elected Bloc MP, Alain Boire, recalled receiving twenty minutes' notice before having to debate the issue of the mountain pine beetle in British Columbia. "Okay, but what's the deal with the mountain pine beetle? I have no idea. I've got to improvise for twenty minutes. And when you're new, it's not so funny," he said.

A handful of MPs, however, relished speaking in the House. "I was the pinch hitter. If [my party] needed someone to make a speech at the last minute, I was always ready. I loved it," said Bloc MP Odina Desrochers.

DESPITE THESE OCCASIONALLY positive sentiments, the former MPs expressed great antipathy for partisan melodramatics and were deeply concerned at how the public perceives politicians in Canada. "Citizens . . . have the impression that politicians are clowns. So they are disaffected, and they lack confidence in their representatives," said Bloc MP Stéphane Bergeron.

"The real sad thing is, at one time, not that many years ago, being a federal Member of Parliament was one of the highest positions you could aspire to," said Conservative MP Jim Gouk. "Now it's right down with lawyers and used-car salesmen. . . . It's interesting because on a personal level I was highly respected in my riding, but in the general sense it's 'You're a politician? Oh my God. Quick! I'm going to hang on to my wallet.'"

Most MPs claimed to regret the partisanship. Discussing personal attacks he made against Liberal Party leader Stéphane Dion, Quebec City Bloc MP Roger Clavet told us: "That man has kids. He has a wife that loves him. When I was in politics, I told myself that I would never stoop so low as to attack him. But I did. I hated him! But today I say, 'My God, his service to this country cost him so much.'"

Our exit interviews suggest that politicians seem to deplore their own public behaviour. They fear it's turning people away from politics. So why not change? If they regretted it so much, why didn't they stop? This disconnect is one aspect of the interviews we found particularly frustrating. MPs rarely took responsibility for their own participation in the behaviour they complained about. If MPs in Question Period demonstrate a behavioural maturity similar to that of a kindergartner, then MPs outside Question Period also exhibit another kindergarten tactic when talking about Question Period: a propensity for finger-pointing and tattletale behaviour that puts the onus for solutions on "those guys." Considering this, we're reminded of Jay Hill's succinct advice to his fellow Conservative MPs: "The only way we will ever get that to stop is [if] enough of you refuse. It's *your*

Members' Statement." Or Question Period answer. Or question. Or whatever.

For the MPs we interviewed, as with the farmers whose sheep grazed freely on the commons in Garrett Hardin's essay, few incentives existed to motivate them to change the political culture they criticized—and many incentives were in place to prevent them from changing. Individual MPs who take a stand face real political costs: from being demoted or removed from committee assignments, to receiving few, if any, opportunities to speak in the House, or being ousted from caucus—or worse. Finally, parties—and particularly the leaders' offices—hold a trump card to guarantee discipline among their ranks: a leader must sign an MP's candidacy papers should he or she wish to run for re-election.

The ugly behaviour is self-perpetuating. The first party to step away from the acrimony takes a risk. Reformers tried to stand above the fray in Parliament after the 1993 election—providing questions to the government in advance so they could prepare thoughtful responses, and rotating seating so their leader, Preston Manning, wasn't always front and centre. It didn't work—they were frequently mocked, and media coverage left them looking undisciplined and unsophisticated. Today, Reform's descendant party, the Conservative Party of Canada, employs tactics to direct and manage MPs' communication as strict as those of any party in Canadian history.

Moving away from insults and ad hominem attacks is something that would work best if all parties moved simultaneously—a near-to-impossible task to coordinate, and a change that no one party is motivated to initiate. So the entrenched partisanship persists, despite the damage it does to the politics, and to the wider public good. It's another example of Hardin's tragedy of the commons.

Finally, the MPs also, inevitably, blamed the media. "For [Question Period] to change sufficiently, to be more of a service to democracy, the media has to change," said Hill. "The media likes it the way it is. There will be columnists who write columns and there will even be reporters who do a short story on what happened in Question Period and how disgusting it is. But the media likes it the way it is because it provides theatre, action, controversy, sells newspapers and it keeps people on that channel on television at night. If it's a boring newscast people are going to flip to a football game or something. So if you want to keep the interest of people, you feel that you have to have some excitement in the House of Commons; people need to be hollering and carrying on like a bunch of imbeciles because it provides good theatre. . . . I think that they are failing Canadians in focusing on ratings and selling newspapers.

"If it is going to change, [the media must] want it to change," Hill continued. "So that if someone is being disruptive and the Speaker—whoever he or she is—tries to do his or her job and reprimands them, the media has to do *its* job; for example, they need . . . to say, 'Pat Martin [Winnipeg NDP MP] was way out of line tonight,' and they have to be on television criticizing his [behaviour], instead of holding him up as some renegade. They have to actually hold him to account."

One thing's certain. Change is necessary because the partisan spiral into which Parliament is descending leads to an increasingly polarized political discourse—which in turn leads to a situation where critical disagreement is marginalized by yelling, and differences of opinion are usurped by drive-by slurs or personal attacks.

Small initial steps could help matters. Take the suggestion of Paul Wells, among others, to make Question Period happen earlier in the day. The logic? Preparation for the partisan battle currently begins once staffers read the morning papers, and continues until the proceedings start at 2:15 p.m. Moving the session up, a few hours, say, so that the proceedings begin every day at 10:00 a.m., has the potential to free up three hours for other, potentially more productive business.

Several MPs looked to the British Parliament for a cure to what ails Canada's Question Period. For example, Montreal Liberal MP Pierre Pettigrew recommended importing the British approach of assigning Cabinet ministers and the prime minister particular days on which they are responsible for answering questions, in hopes that rotation would produce a more substantial exchange. "In Canada, we monopolize the whole government every day. You have thirty minutes, with thirty ministers held hostage five days a week. It's ridiculous," he said.

But the largest category of Question Period–related recommendations involved the Chamber's culture of antagonism, which MPs felt alienated citizens from politics writ large as well as from the pursuit of political office. An MP who was a former teacher, Myron Thompson, suggested the Speaker should enforce better behaviour, the way Thompson once enforced classroom respect and congeniality. Other MPs believed the change should start at the top, said Ken Epp, Edmonton Conservative MP. "I really would like to see party leaders from all parties engage in sober debate, and not throwing the malicious barbs back and forth," he recommended. And of course, the existing culture is perpetuated by negative political advertising, which is currently heavily underwritten by tax credits and subsidies, and produced without requiring leaders or candidates to stand publicly by their messages. It may very well be time to implement Andrew Coyne's suggestions to terminate this subsidization, or to instill greater accountability by making political leaders authorize, or even voice-over, any attack ads their party commissions. Or, to go even further, maybe tax-deductible donations should not be allowable for this type of advertising, in the spirit that the public purse should not be used to undermine constructive and necessary debate.

"It [the behaviour] could be changed by politicians tomorrow if they decided not to do it," said NDP MP Bill Blaikie. "[But] the reward is to be left out of the story and to be left out of the story is like you're not there. And to look like you are not there is to look like you're not doing your job. So publicity becomes a kind of a substitute for achievement. What do you measure? Well, you measure, 'Did you get on the *National*?' 'Did you get in the media?' And yet the things that are the most important over the years were things that were often achieved obscurely."

Where there may be a glimmer of hope is if MPs buck the current trends. If MPs stop blaming each other for their histrionics in the House. If they stop blaming the media. If they stop blaming the Speaker's inability, or unwillingness, to police the place appropriately. At some point, we hope MPs stand up and take responsibility for their own behaviour.

Bill Blaikie, an MP for over twenty-nine years, might have put it best. "The real scandal is that the place is seized so often with scandals and alleged scandals," he said. "That is the scandal. You're down in the corner talking about whether we are going to be able to drink the water or breathe the air or grow plants in the soil by the year 2030—and all they're concerned about is who gave what contract to whom. It's not that corruption doesn't matter; it's just there is something ultimately not corrupt but something *wrong* about being obsessed by those issues, and those alone, both on the part of whatever Members of Parliament are obsessed by it, and on the part of the media that constantly feed this thing. That's the most frustrating. That is what drove me wild and still does—of all the things that we should actually be putting our heart and soul into. Instead, it's the sandbox."

CHAPTER SIX

Where the Real Work Gets Done (Sometimes)

C anada was a fiscal mess in the early '90s. By 1995 the federal debt was $554.2 billion, thanks to the budget deficits that governments allowed from 1980 to 1995. The trend began with Pierre Trudeau's Liberals in the early '80s, and despite progress in reducing the deficit under Progressive Conservative governments led primarily by Brian Mulroney, the debt itself continued to rise into the Jean Chrétien era, which began in 1993. Through that time the federal debt as a share of the economy grew from 46.9 percent in 1985–86 to 68.4 percent in 1995–96. At that point, servicing the debt represented the government's single largest expenditure—it cost 36 cents of every dollar spent. The accumulation of borrowing led international capital markets to examine the fundamental stability of the Canadian economy.

When the Mexican peso collapsed in December 1994, an international crisis loomed. Some in Ottawa interpreted the event as a warning. The Reform Party called for action on the debt, as did Canada's banks and a series of think tanks.

But what really triggered change was an editorial in the *Wall Street Journal* on January 12, 1995. "Mexico isn't the only U.S. neighbor flirting with the financial abyss," the editorial began. "Turn around and check out Canada, which has now become an honorary member of the Third World in the unmanageability of its debt problem."

Nothing focuses Canada's attention more than seeing its name in an international headline. To prevent the sort of financial calamity that has since befallen countries like Greece and Russia, then finance minister Paul Martin set to work on a budget that would come to define a new age of financial responsibility for the Canadian government. "Mr. Speaker," he began his budget speech of February 27, 1995, "there are times . . . when fundamental challenges must be faced, fundamental choices made—a new course charted. For Canada, this is one of those times." Martin's 1995 budget proposed spending cuts of $25 billion. It shrank the federal government by 45,000 employees over the following three years. The $15.3 billion the federal government paid out to finance unemployment benefits annually was to decline by 10 percent. The budget cut federal transfers to the provinces to finance welfare programs. Even old age pensions were not spared.

Remarkably, given the extent of the cuts, the Liberal government's approval rating rose by five points—from 58 percent to 63 percent—in the wake of the budget, according to an Angus Reid Group poll, and two out of three of the people surveyed indicated they approved of the budget.

So how did Martin do it? One helpful factor was that both major opposition parties, the Bloc and Reform, favoured radical spending cuts. After Martin tabled the budget, both parties criticized the Liberals for not cutting enough. But in his exit interview, Martin himself credited the efforts of the finance committee led by Toronto-area Liberal MP Jim Peterson with helping to sell the 1995 budget. Knowing that circumstances required a federal financial plan, Martin assigned Peterson's committee a stage-setting role. They were to travel the country gleaning ideas on what to do—knowing that the meetings would also inform people how dire Canada's situation was.

"Don't meet with the business community alone," Martin recalled telling Peterson. "Hold public meetings—but don't meet with the business community alone, don't meet with the First Nations alone, don't meet with the educators alone. You have them all come to the table so that when the business community says, 'You have got to cut taxes, therefore cut social programs,' and the unions say, 'You've got to increase social programs and increase taxes'—people saw the tradeoffs they were forced to make. The committee did a tremendous job."

Beginning in mid-October with a deadline to report to Parliament on December 7, 1994, Peterson's multi-partisan finance committee began "pre-budget hearings," which provided an opportunity for citizens to advise Ottawa how to reduce its $40 billion deficit. It was an informed group. Among the fourteen fellow committee members were the economists Stephen Harper and Herb Grubel, both Reform Party members, as well as the Liberal lawyer and committee vice-chair Barry Campbell, and the Bloc economist and vice-chair Yvan Loubier. Among the witnesses testifying before the committee were some impressive luminaries, recalled Peterson. "We had seventeen or eighteen of the most important stakeholders in the country. . . . Business, labour,

NGOs—we had presentations and I breathed a sigh of relief because at the end of it, every one of them said we had to do something with the deficit. Now there was absolutely no agreement on what should have to be cut. Or how to do it. But when you had unanimity coming out of that incredible group of leading Canadian thinkers, it gave a tremendous boost to the concept that we had to deal with this."

Pension experts told Peterson and his committee not to tax RRSPs or pensions. Others argued against taxing company-sponsored health plans. In fact, everyone who came in seemed to have suggestions about where *not* to cut. By mid-November, Peterson commented sardonically, few of the witnesses had offered any suggestions about where *to* cut. "Most of the witnesses are very self-serving," he observed, describing a paradox in the consensus he was hearing. Don't raise taxes, people told him. But do cut the deficit.

The finance committee's December report recommended a combination of cuts and tax hikes. But public response was unequivocal. The report set off what the *Wall Street Journal* called a "spontaneous tax revolt." Call-in radio shows and newspaper editorialists came out against any new taxes. Martin had the momentum he needed to convince the Cabinet that any deficit-cutting needed to happen through spending reductions.

Once Martin released his budget in February 1995, the *Wall Street Journal* did a one-eighty and applauded: "Canada's bold budget ought to be an inspiration to other countries struggling with overextended governments." While Canadian reactions were more muted, an editorial in *La Presse* hailed "a welcome return to realistic public spending," and the *Globe and Mail* expressed relief that "the government [had] avoided a crisis." Almost two decades later, even an organization as loath to praise Liberals as the Fraser Institute lauds the 1995 Martin budget as "a defining moment in Canada's fiscal history."

IN PAUL MARTIN'S judgment, it was Peterson's 1994–95 finance committee that prepared the ground for Canada's most important budget—which has been credited with rescuing the Canadian economy and giving the impetus for our current reputation as a relative paragon of global financial responsibility. It is highly unusual that anyone should credit a parliamentary committee with such a feat. Unlike that finance committee, which was assigned extensive and high-profile consultations, most committees in Ottawa pass unremarked, attract scant media attention and are attended only by a few stakeholder groups. The general public rarely notices.

It is understandable that Martin would so effusively praise committee work in our interview—he was simply giving credit where credit is due. But he wasn't alone. The majority of our interviewees emphasized that some of the best and most productive work on Parliament Hill took place in committees, as well as in the off-the-record, closed-door gatherings of MPs known as caucuses. It was in committees and caucuses that MPs could collaborate, debating and advancing policy, and bringing local issues to the national stage. "Committee is where the work gets done," said Walt Lastewka, Liberal MP for St. Catharines, echoing a sentiment expressed by many of his colleagues. "The majority of work in Ottawa is done in committees. A lot of people don't realize that," said fellow Ontario Liberal Pat O'Brien.

We were taken by surprise that former MPs so frequently cited committee work as a highlight of their political careers. Committees don't always get such glowing reviews. One doesn't need to read *Dilbert* to know that, in many office cultures, they are seen as administrative graveyards where ideas are buried in endless discussion. In Parliament, it seems, committee work has an entirely different reputation. "We dealt with real issues, very substantive issues, and we came to grips with some real problems," said Werner Schmidt, the Conservative MP from B.C. He also stressed their cross-partisan approach. "If a good idea comes forward from the NDP, fine. If a good idea comes from a Liberal, fine. . . . If it is the right position, I am not going to oppose it. Why would I do that?" he said. "The feeling of the committee [is that] we are here to do a job . . . and then, what can we do to bring this together?"

Because committees and caucuses do tend to exist "under the radar," members' repeatedly expressed enthusiasm for them is hard to assess independently. Are committees really all they're cracked up to be, or is it just that they are more effective than what's on display in the House of Commons? Dale Johnston, former Conservative MP for the Alberta riding of Wetaskiwin, hinted that the latter might be the case. "Committees are good because there's a genuine desire to get things done," he said, implying that other, more public, areas of parliamentary business are less productive. Werner Schmidt agreed: "What is portrayed in the mass media is Question Period and not committee work. Question Period is the theatre of Parliament. It's not where the work gets done. It's where the voting takes place, but it is not where the work is done. The real work of Parliament is done in committees."

Whatever the reason, if the purported "best work" of Parliament takes place away from the public gaze, how are Canadians to observe and understand the work of their elected representatives—not to mention hold MPs accountable? So just what happens inside committees? What makes them so effective? Whatever happens to their reports and studies? And can we learn anything from them that is relevant to other aspects of life on Parliament Hill?

NEARLY EVERY MP IS expected to serve on at least one committee—a multi-party group of parliamentarians who are charged with considering a particular item of legislation, in addition to various policies and program areas. According to the House of Commons Compendium:

> Committee work provides detailed information to parliamentarians on issues of concern to the electorate and often provokes important public debate. In addition, because committees interact directly with the public, they provide an immediate and visible conduit between elected representatives and Canadians. Committees are extensions of the House, created by either standing or special orders, and are limited in their powers by the authority delegated to them.

Party whips decide which MPs are placed on which committees. Committee seats are apportioned according to the distribution of the seats in the House. Each committee has a chair who is elected by the members of the committee. The committee chair is usually drawn from the governing party. Each committee also has two vice-chairs, one drawn from the Official Opposition and the other from another opposition party.

Deliberation and consultation by a committee often contributes to the passage of a legislative act from bill into law. In these cases, after a bill reaches second reading, the proposed legislation is dispatched to be considered either by a standing committee, such as finance, or by a committee struck purely for the purpose of considering the effects of that specific bill. Various experts and interested parties are called to testify about the proposed legislation in hearings before the committee; and once testimony closes, committee members collaborate to consider, propose and recommend amendments to the bill.

As the Compendium indicates, committee proceedings are ostensibly public, but in practice they're rarely covered by the media. Perhaps for that reason, and in contrast to the theatrics of the House, the MPs said committees were marked by collegiality and constructive debate. In committees they immerse themselves in the details of proposed legislation and propose amendments, or study and report to the House on emerging issues. "You are fighting all the time, but it's a sparring that's at a level where you want to get a good report," said Liberal MP Bill Graham.

The presentations of witnesses before committees allow the Canadian public at large to have a say in committee work. "We were always meeting with groups, which was tremendously helpful in terms of getting to understand the issues that people were concerned about around the country," said Conservative MP Monte Solberg. Travel in areas potentially affected by a certain legislation was another excellent way to gain citizen input and allow MPs to craft legislation that better reflected citizens' needs. One MP who chaired the agriculture committee recalled the importance of visiting farmers directly. "We toured the country, bringing forward a series of recommendations and offering help to provinces who were in difficulty with agriculture. We met with people, and saw how agriculture [had] changed," said former Liberal MP Charles Hubbard.

Former MPs attributed the productivity of committees in part to their largely non-partisan environment. "Committees are where most relationships get established. You sit there for at least four or five hours a week with the same individuals. You find out who they are through their questions, their ideas, and you develop respect for them," said Liberal MP Omar Alghabra. And, Graham noted, committees require MPs to "take off their partisan hats and say, 'Okay, we are going to work on something here to get the best possible thing we can for the country, recognizing we have different political attitudes.'"

MPs recalled committees as a place where diverse perspectives and expert knowledge were gathered. They represented a venue for expert witnesses to provide context to legislation's potential effects. "We bring in the best experts in the world, we deliberate over the important issues of the day. It's quite something. If you were to come and watch, I think you would go away thinking, 'Wow, this is good. My country is in good hands,'" said the late Liberal MP Andy Scott.

The committee system isn't perfect, however, and when pressed, some MPs admitted they had real concerns about committees' effectiveness. Take Scott's experience. Scott was a New Brunswick Liberal who came to Parliament as an MP for the first time in 1993. His field of expertise was literacy and skills training, the area in which he had worked in Fredericton as a senior policy advisor to New Brunswick premier Frank McKenna. Soon after he first arrived in Ottawa, Scott was surprised to hear he'd been placed on the health committee—surprised, he said, because he didn't know anything about health care. "I should be on the human resources committee," Scott insisted, to no avail. "I was baffled that it didn't seem to matter." Many MPs mentioned a similar frustration that their initial committee appointments were unexpected or unsuitable, and did not match their experience or interests.

Making the appointment process even more arbitrary was the fact that, regardless of party, MPs found they had no formal opportunity to request a particular policy focus, and no recourse if they considered a particular committee appointment inappropriate or not of interest. "I couldn't go to somebody and say, 'Look, you've got me on the wrong committee,'" Scott said. Scott began to feel the extent of the party's control over him. He realized that to the parties' decision-makers, the interests and experience of individual members perhaps didn't matter all that much. In Fredericton he would have spoken up and been moved the next day. But in Ottawa, he realized, things were different. "That wasn't the way it worked. 'You're on a committee because that's where we put you and don't worry if you don't know enough about it; we are going to give you notes anyway.'"

Liberal MP Andrew Telegdi was similarly confounded by the process. "They put me on the public accounts committee. I was not keen on being on public accounts," he said, naming a committee that reviews the work of the auditor general, among other matters. "I couldn't get myself changed."

He ended up becoming the committee's vice-chair. It was on this committee that Telegdi witnessed what he regarded as an egregious mismanagement of human resources. Despite its topic, the public accounts committee had only two chartered accountants among its members, one of whom was Liberal MP Alex Shepherd. Shepherd, however, had voted against the wishes of the party leadership on gun registry legislation, and as punishment, according to Telegdi, the party higher-ups took him out of public accounts—leaving only one accountant on the committee. "It didn't make any sense," said Telegdi, who believed the move "weakened the committee."

"If I would fault my leaders," said former Liberal MP Sue Barnes, "I never felt that they'd learned our backgrounds. And it was funny because if you were put on a justice committee, you were thought of as a justice person, when maybe your expertise was in health. People in your caucus saw you as what you were working on, and sometimes it was a match, and sometimes it wasn't. Sometimes it was a pigeon-hole that people never escaped."

Another problematic observation was that for all the talk about the level of the debate and expertise, committees didn't much affect policy and legislation. Conservative MP Randy White put it bluntly: "People will tell you 'I've done great work on a committee.' But you really have to say, 'You did good work. You travelled. You studied this and that. But what did you accomplish? Show us where the legislation changed and what you did.'"

Other MPs commented that the work of committees wasn't adequately integrated into the government decision-making process. For this reason, former Conservative MP Inky

Mark, for one, complained that committees weren't productive components of the legislative process. "Waste a lot of money, waste a lot of time," said Mark. "I mean, we study and study and study things to death and they become nice packages to collect dust. It [policy] does not change."

Several factors contribute to such lack of productivity, as reported by the MPs we interviewed, many of whom had served in minority Parliaments. Elections could be called at any time, bringing an end to committee deliberations, studies or reports. Or the recommendations of a committee might be at odds with governmental priorities. Liberal Marlene Catterall, for instance, said that few committees studying emerging issues produce budget estimates, making implementation of their recommendations more difficult. Others noted that the governing party is only required to respond to a report within a hundred and twenty days and is not obliged to act on a committee's advice in any substantial way. Catterall believed committees could do far more to push the adoption of their recommendations: "Committees should take the government's response, critique it and then publicize those views," she said.

Tenure and experience are important to committee work, we heard. The longer MPs served together on a committee, the better they got to know each other, and the better they worked together. The significance of tenure, beyond being part of a "team," is that MPs can become topic experts. This expertise helps them create or debate policy more thoroughly—which, in turn, makes them better MPs and makes it more likely that their work will have influence.

Some of our interviewees, however, deplored the fact that party leadership ignored the potential benefits of tenure.

As they described the proceedings, it became clear that many believed committees had become a tool for party leadership to exert control over individual MPs. Leaders could disrupt and subvert the committee process, replacing MPs without notice or consultation. For committee proceedings that the Prime Minister's Office (PMO) found politically sensitive, musical-chairs machinations were typical. Conservative MP Ken Epp recounted an occasion, for instance, when the governing Liberal Party replaced all its members just before an amendment vote. "Some committees I was on, we had members of the committee, we listened to witnesses, we would come up with agreements on amendments, and the day of the vote on clause by clause the whip substitutes every member of the committee on the government side," Epp said. "They're out and a new bunch of guys are in whose only qualification is that they will vote the way they're told. They haven't been there for the debates. They haven't heard the arguments. They haven't allowed themselves to be persuaded. All they are is obedient to the cause." His recommendation? "I would like to see that changed. I would like to see the committees have independence from their party whips and we would get better legislation."

The musical-chairs phenomenon was particularly characteristic of committee proceedings that were due to be televised. "Debates are much more reasonable in committees that aren't televised," said Liberal MP Paul DeVillers. "You televise a committee and you get the same nonsense; you don't get the usual members of the committee. Parties substitute their hitters to come into the committee when it's a televised committee, as opposed to the people who are there normally, doing the work." (Most committee proceedings are now webcast.) Paul Martin agreed. "Televising committees is just absolutely the worst thing in the world because all of a sudden the attempt at non-partisanship, the attempt to be reasonable, goes out the window," he said. Another deplorable thing that happens, he added, is that substitute members are intentionally placed on committees as "verbal assassins" with a mission "to attack people personally if their views are different."

Meddling of this sort is damaging to MPs' cross-party working relationships. "One of the things that would be ideal would be for the parliamentary secretaries not to sit on the committee," said Conservative MP Monte Solberg. "The parliamentary secretaries for the various ministers will, with a wink and a nudge, tell the government members what position to take. And I don't think that's helpful in the end. It removes some of the independence of the committees and once it's perceived to be the case that the government is trying to jam something through, then the goodwill evaporates and any relationships that you have become secondary to advancing your party. So that's probably the single biggest thing that could be done."

Party whips can also grant or withhold assignments to sought-after committee posts as a means of rewarding or punishing more junior MPs. "One of the ways in which the whips have control over you as a Member," said Bill Graham, "is they can approve your travel and they can approve your committee position. Everybody wanted to be on the foreign affairs committee, but if you didn't play ball you were out of there and you could go and sit on the library committee for the rest of your life."

Graham and Martin were the two party leaders we interviewed who said they supported continuity in committee membership through the duration of a Parliament to protect committee work from partisan interference. "I am a strong proponent of that reform," said Bill Graham. "You are appointed to the committee and you're there for the duration of the Parliament. That preserves the integrity of the committee system."

IF COMMITTEES ARE effectively private for lack of media attention and public interest, caucus is private by design. The term "caucus" has several different meanings in Canadian political life. It can refer to a group of MPs from a given party gathered to discuss and formulate the party's official position on a given topic. While Parliament is in session each party holds a meeting of MPs for this purpose at least weekly. Caucus is the "belly of the beast"—the space where MPs are closest to their party. If the party directs the MPs' actions on the floor of the House, said the MPs in our interviews, then it was in caucus that they had a chance to turn things around and influence party policy. Only MPs, senators and a few senior political staff attend caucus meetings; members of the public service, the media and the general public are typically refused entry. And by convention, what takes place in caucus is off the record and not to be discussed outside the party (although leaks are not uncommon).

The term "caucus" also applies to the more informal but remarkably effective groups within a party that meet to provide input on, and to develop policy in specific areas. Smaller caucuses can be created to address any area of interest or issue, to focus on specific regions, or to advance the interests of a particular group. There are also caucuses about a single topic—an auto caucus, for example. In some cases, a multi-party caucus can be set up to bring together MPs from different political parties who share a common interest.

The off-the-record nature of caucuses allows members the freedom to discuss how they really feel about an issue. Some of the debates can be off-colour, and the debating can be spirited, interviewees said. "One thing about our caucus—there were drag-me-out debates. You've got people with one opinion, people with the totally opposite opinion and you try and meet in the middle. It's a huge, huge thing," said Conservative MP Carol Skelton, who credited Prime Minister Stephen Harper with great skill at bringing his caucus to consensus. "He's really, really good. The PM stays there for the whole caucus meeting. He's always there. He'll get right into it, too. Basically at the end you come out with a consensus. It might take you the whole time, but you come out with a consensus."

"[Caucus] was probably the most stimulating part of my career," said Liberal MP Roy Cullen. "When I got to Ottawa, I went to my first caucus meeting and the debate was so intense I turned to a colleague and said, 'Is it always like this?'"

Despite the intensity of the exchanges, however, some MPs were dissatisfied by the little control they had over the process that turned the "variance of opinion" voiced during caucus meetings into the official party line. "You discuss and discuss and discuss, but there's no consensus. But the leader has to leave for the media scrum . . . and so he would say, 'We're going to make a consensus on this, this and this. All agreed?' We didn't have time to discuss it. And that's 'consensus,'" said Bloc MP Odina Desrochers.

"I have often compared it to a family," said former Liberal MP Marlene Catterall of a party's caucus. In 2001

Catterall became Ottawa's first female chief whip, and played that role for more than two years in the Chrétien government, in addition to serving six years as deputy whip. "We could have all the discussions we want about where we are going on holidays this year. But once the family makes a decision, the family is going together on a holiday."

To Catterall, the good functioning of the whip is integral to the operation of a healthy caucus. "You try, and let people know that you are trying to make sure that they have a role they can play that is important to them, and they can make a real contribution through their committee work," Catterall said. "That is for starters. Secondly you listen to them when they have a concern about something coming to the House, and you see if there is any way of accommodating what they are concerned about.

"I happen to feel I have had the experience of working in a very democratic caucus," Catterall added. "When we were in government, there was something I wanted to accomplish, something I wanted to get done. And the first question from the senior policy advisor was, do you have caucus onside? Because if you can have caucus onside you can have just about anything, and if you don't, it's a tough sell. And that says to me a lot about the importance of caucus to [Prime Minister Chrétien].

"From then on, any time I wanted to do something, any time I wanted the minister to change his or her mind about something, that's what I did, whether it was the local Eastern Ontario caucus, Ontario caucus, the women's caucus, the particular policy committee of caucus. I worked it because I knew that was what would get the minister and the prime minister onside." Or as Liberal MP Ken Boshcoff put it, "The route to change is through the internal caucus system."

"Some of it is quite formal," recalled Conservative MP Chuck Strahl. "When you have major initiatives you actually have a group that you talk to before you mention a big important initiative. So if you are agriculture minister, you will have a group of agriculture-invested caucus members, maybe a dozen of them or twenty of them even, and you are expected to meet with them once a month. You talk to them and then move ahead on changes—to the Wheat Board, for example. 'Are you guys okay with that?' 'Does anybody see a problem with that?' So actually it's quite formal. You are expected to do that [consult]—and if you don't do it, often you won't be allowed to bring [a proposal] to Cabinet. You are expected to tell people at Cabinet level what the caucus thinks about it. [The process is] quite formal, and actually to the point where, if you can't check that box, if you can't say, 'I have talked to my support group or my internal group,' if you say, 'Oh, I just forgot to do that this time,'—they will say, 'Well, bring it back next month—you are off the agenda.' So in our party, at least, it was quite formal and quite strict. You either could display caucus support or you could not bring it forward."

Backbench MPs could affect policy in informal ways, Strahl added. "At every moment of every caucus meeting, Question Period—[even] time when you're sitting alone in your thoughts—caucus members are not shy about buttonholing you as a minister to tell you what you should be doing. . . . There is a lot of ongoing consultation. Some of it is formal letters and stuff, but backbench MPs on the government side have many opportunities every week to bend the ear of ministers on whatever they want, and so you just have to be available. . . . You are just there and they have complete access to you, there is no running away and if they want a meeting, a more formal meeting—you are expected to do that as well. [Because] no minister wants to be in the room when somebody gets up to a microphone, and says to the prime minister, 'I just can't seem to get a meeting with that agriculture minister.' I mean, that is a bad moment; you just do not want that, because that is a career-limiting move. That is how serious that is. If your reputation is you are not approachable, and the prime minister hears about it a few times . . .? You can have walking papers."

One case study that reflects the organic but no less effective nature of caucus fomentation and action is the story of the late '90s post-secondary education caucus that existed within the Chrétien government. By 1997–98, Paul Martin's cuts in federal government spending had helped turned the feds' budget deficit into a $3 billion surplus. But the cuts came with a cost—a 24 percent cut to what provincial transfers had been two years earlier. Ontario was particularly hard hit, as Progressive Conservative premier Mike Harris followed the decreases in federal-provincial transfers with $1 billion in provincial-education spending cuts, including a 14.3 percent decrease in funding to Ontario universities.

Within the federal Liberal caucus there was a lot of concern about the effects the spending cuts would have on the nation's universities—particularly among the MPs who represented electoral districts that contained institutions of higher education. An entity called the "post-secondary education caucus" had already been founded by three Liberal MPs, of whom two also happened to be academics—Peter Adams of

Peterborough, which included Trent University where Adams had been a geography professor, and John English of Kitchener, a history professor at the University of Waterloo, whose riding included Wilfrid Laurier University. The third founder was Andrew Telegdi, who also represented a Kitchener-Waterloo riding from 1993 until 2008.

As Telegdi recalls it, the impetus for the post-secondary education caucus was Jean Chrétien's first Throne Speech, on January 19, 1994, in which the new prime minister had neglected to make a single mention of research. "We essentially said that we [were] going to make sure that this doesn't happen again, [and] we put higher education right in front and centre," Telegdi recalled.

"There were upwards of thirty of us in it," recalled Peter Adams in his exit interview. Members joined, he said, "either from background interest or because of their ridings, particularly the small Maritime ridings where they've got a tiny university . . . and the people locally see them as economic drivers. So we set up this thing while the cuts were going through and we began work almost immediately."

"To me the best investment you can ever make is higher education and supporting research and development," says Telegdi. "Basically, we set up an organization that would have all the Members of Parliament that had universities in their ridings. We started with that group and we actually expanded from that so even people who didn't have a post-secondary institution in their constituency, but lived close to it, would end up joining. So it became probably one of the largest caucuses. . . . And then we had the Cabinet ministers added [to] our meetings, and we always made sure that the issues were front and centre, and we would always meet with them before budget time to remind them that we don't want to go back to the old days."

In Canada, education is the responsibility of the provincial governments. But thanks to the attention the federal Liberal caucus drew to the issue, the Chrétien government moved to create mechanisms that allowed it to inject funding into the nation's universities. The additional funding created such organizations as the Canadian Institutes of Health Research, the Canadian Foundation for Innovation and the Canada Research Chair program, designed to help the nation's universities attract research talent from around the world. Another initiative from the period was the Canadian Millennium Scholarship Foundation, which was established in 1998 and ran for ten years with a federal government contribution of $2.5 billion to improve access to post-secondary education.

Despite that first Throne Speech, post-secondary education became one of Jean Chrétien's most important legacies, thanks in part to the efforts of the post-secondary education caucus. "The most far-sighted policy of the Chrétien years benefited the university sector, an ironic legacy for a prime minister not known for his cerebral interests," observed Jeffrey Simpson in a feature-length assessment of the Chrétien legacy in 2003, the year he resigned. "These programs better equipped Canada for competing in the world of knowledge."

"We [helped] the higher education and research community on how to cope with the cuts," said Peter Adams, looking back. "Some terrific changes came through. You know, the huge research foundations, grants for the indirect costs of research, these are obscure [but] very, very important things.

They all had to do with productivity in the country, and the strength of the influence of the federal government. . . . By the time we finished, we had representatives from the professors' unions, the student unions, the presidents and directors of the universities coming to us." Adams believes that the caucus drove at least $16 billion in funding to universities and university research, and possibly as much as $20 billion—not a bad result for Telegdi, Adams and English, each of whom was a backbench MP when they founded the caucus.

PAUL MARTIN'S ACKNOWLEDGEMENT of the influence of Jim Peterson's 1994–95 finance committee stands as one of the few examples of an established political leader giving credit to a relatively under-recognized aspect of the legislative process, the committee, for its major and beneficial impact on important Canadian policy. The same credit could be extended to Adams, Telegdi and English's post-secondary education caucus. (We recognize that both these examples come from Liberal MPs; for whatever reason, the Liberals proved to be far more effusive about committees and caucuses than their political peers.)

We don't hear enough about committees, and we certainly don't hear enough about caucuses. The sense of satisfaction the MPs described with their work on committees and in caucus stood in marked contrast to their frustration with other parts of their jobs. But even then, MPs reported having their appointments and efforts thwarted by the party's hand, and seeing committee memberships and proceedings manipulated or truncated to fit party agendas. This is troubling in itself: again, why should Parliament dedicate so many hours and resources to a process if it isn't designed to work? Shouldn't we be troubled that the most effective work the MPs described had to be carried out almost entirely away from public notice, in rarely watched committees or the closed-door spaces of caucus?

PERHAPS WE SHOULD expect that parliamentary productivity should increase in proportion to the venue's privacy. After all, few workplaces see their proceedings on the public record, allowing public examination of on-the-job mistakes. In order for productive work to take place, it is perhaps natural for MPs to seek out spaces where they are not constantly required to perform. On the other hand, few workplaces feature as wide-ranging an effect on citizens' day-to-day lives as Parliament, and it's unfortunate that so much of what Canadians see or have explained to them is often facile debate and finger-pointing on the floor of the House.

Former MPs told us that they liked caucus and believed, in general, that private party forums represented productive places for backbench MPs to voice their opinions and influence party policy. Caucuses are tricky to criticize or praise in a general manner. So many are idiosyncratic to their own particular leader; if the leader is good at creating consensus out of many disparate viewpoints then individual MPs will feel they're contributing in caucus and are valued by the party and leadership. We couldn't help noticing how many MPs professed that their own particular leader was excellent at building consensus in caucus; but any residual partisanship aside, it certainly appears that caucuses form an under-appreciated component to our democracy and the role MPs play in it.

The benefits of committees to the healthy functioning of Canada's democracy are a little less clear. MPs said they conducted good, multi-partisan work in committee. However, many of them said this good work failed to have any substantial effect on legislation or policy, and that party control often thwarted members' best efforts.

Most organizations try to take advantage of their teams' strengths; in contrast, it's troubling to hear about political parties' apparent disregard for placing individual MPs on appropriate committees—seemingly blind to the obvious value of having a chartered accountant on the public accounts committee, for instance. Why would a party clear out committee members when the MPs begin to develop expertise in a subject and start to develop policy opinions of their own? Such practices suggest that MPs aren't placed on a committee to work with MPs from other parties to create the best legislation for Canada. They aren't there to exert their expertise. The MPs are there to further the interests of party leadership. It's yet another example of leadership treating individual MPs as little more than expensive voting machines, on Parliament Hill to simply do as the leader's office tells them.

CHAPTER SEVEN

Living in the Franchise

From the thoughts shared by the MPs we interviewed, a picture emerged of the extent of party domination in Ottawa. In managing the nomination process for prospective MPs, in providing direction to MPs, and in committees and in caucuses we've seen that political parties and their leaders prefer members who demonstrate loyalty and adhere to party lines, above all other values. This expectation allows parties to appear organized and cohesive to the electorate.

So, what happens when an MP disagrees with the party?

That's the question Joe Comuzzi was forced to confront one Wednesday in January 2005, after he left a Liberal Party caucus meeting in Fredericton, New Brunswick. He returned to his hotel room, lay down on the bed, stared at the ceiling and thought.

He spent an hour in that position, thinking about his career as an MP, and about the constituency that sent him to Ottawa. For seventeen years Comuzzi had been a good soldier in the Liberal Party. First elected in 1988, the MP for Thunder Bay–Superior North, a lifelong Catholic, a former car salesman known on Parliament Hill for his impeccable dress and his 6' 4" stature, voted consistently with his party even when he didn't want to. Take federal minister of health Allan Rock's controversial tainted-blood policy. Rock's policy would only compensate people who had been infected by hepatitis C between 1986 and 1990, leaving uncompensated anyone who had been infected by tainted blood earlier. In April 1998 the opposition Reform Party tried to extend the coverage, and the Liberals closed ranks to support Rock's original policy.

Comuzzi recalled the "pounding in caucus" that required Liberal MPs to vote against the Reform Party's resolution. Privately, Comuzzi figured that the opposition was right. And he knew other Liberals felt the same way. He saw them gritting their teeth as they stood up to vote against the motion, sticking with the party line. Comuzzi also voted against Reform's motion. "I shouldn't have," Comuzzi said. Even though Ontario premier Mike Harris eventually passed legislation to compensate that province's victims who were infected earlier than 1986, Comuzzi would later say that he wished he could take back his vote.

But the toughest decision Comuzzi ever faced was the one he was mulling over in his Fredericton hotel room. The big topic at the caucus retreat was the impending legislation over gay marriage. Prime Minister Paul Martin told his Liberal caucus that he would allow backbench MPs to vote according to their conscience. The only members of the Liberal caucus required to support gay marriage were those in Cabinet.

Hence Comuzzi's bind: he was a Cabinet member. Like any politician, he'd always wanted a spot in Cabinet. He'd been a loyal Liberal MP for sixteen years when, less than a year earlier, the prime minister handed him his first Cabinet position. The title was a mouthful: the minister of state for the federal economic development initiative for northern Ontario. The position was an endorsement of Comuzzi's career, a sign of his respect in the party, an indication of his stature as an elder statesman.

Comuzzi had quit smoking that December. Then stress over the impending gay marriage vote prompted him to return to the habit. Gay marriage was not popular in his comparatively conservative riding of Thunder Bay. It certainly was not popular with the Catholic Church—and Comuzzi, educated in a Catholic boarding school, was an ardent adherent to the religion. During the 2004 campaign for his most recent election win, Comuzzi had promised his constituents that he would vote to uphold the traditional definition of marriage. So Comuzzi could vote the way he promised, the way his conscience and his constituents wanted him to—or he could keep his Cabinet position. "Is it worth giving up a Cabinet post over?" he mused to the *Globe and Mail* at the time.

Justice Minister Irwin Cotler introduced the gay marriage legislation, Bill C-38, on February 1, 2005. To decide how he'd vote on it, Comuzzi spent six weeks travelling around his mostly rural riding. Towns like McKenna, Geraldton, Longlac, Nipigon, Red Rock—Comuzzi visited them all, holding open forums in each place and taking notes as he gauged how his constituents wanted him to vote. "I wanted to know what they thought about it," Comuzzi said. "It's a private affair and I've always considered it that. But when it came to making that decision, I voted in my mind that it was a consensus of the people that I represented, that wanted me to vote that way."

On the basis of what he heard from his constituents, Comuzzi decided he had to vote against the bill. He wasn't the only one. (MP Pat O'Brien also left the Liberal caucus over same-sex marriage and opted to sit as an Independent.) So on the morning of Tuesday, June 28, 2005, Comuzzi had a conversation with the prime minister. Comuzzi told Martin he was resigning from Cabinet in order to vote against gay marriage, as his constituents wished. The prime minister told him that he was disappointed. "I very much regret the decision," Martin told the *Globe and Mail.* "But I understand it, and accept it." Martin said he was delighted, however, that Comuzzi would continue to serve as a Liberal Member of Parliament and a strong advocate for northern Ontario.

That afternoon, Comuzzi voted against Bill C-38's third reading. The legislation passed, 158–133. It also passed in the Senate, and became law on July 20, 2005, making Canada the third country in the world at that time to legalize gay marriage, behind only Belgium and the Netherlands, and the first in the Americas. "I promised faithfully to the people of Thunder Bay–Superior North that I would defend the traditional definition of marriage," Comuzzi said. Once he realized what his constituents wanted him to do, he did it. "It was an easy decision."

The press lauded Comuzzi. "Quietly, without fanfare or negotiation, he resigned his junior ministry and voted against same-sex [marriage] through personal conviction and a commitment he had made to the people who elected him—an act almost without parallel in this grasping generation of career politicians," wrote Bruce Garvey in the *National Post.* "He not only said what he would do and then did it; he put public interest ahead of his own when the moment came to decide," said the *Toronto Star*'s James Travers. "By stepping aside, by giving up something cherished for an even more precious principle, Comuzzi accepted the uncompromising discipline of public service."

COMUZZI'S DILEMMA INVOLVED one of the key tensions in the life of a Canadian MP—the triangular relationship between constituency wishes, personal opinion and party loyalty. It's hard enough to figure out what constituents want, particularly since they're unlikely to all have the same perspectives or demands. But under the pressure of one of Ottawa's unwritten rules, that tension is even more difficult to manage. Adhere to the party line, goes the unspoken edict from the leader's office, particularly on the decisions for which we need you, and we'll pay you back. We'll help you in your riding. Whether it's working to arrange funding for a new jobs program, or a technology office park, a new manufacturing facility or federal infrastructure funding—the governing party can and will assist the good soldiers. By voting against his party on Bill C-38, a vote his constituents requested, Comuzzi did something that harmed his standing within his party and likely weakened his ability to direct federal money to the riding of Thunder Bay–Superior North.

"It's a trade-off," Comuzzi said in his exit interview, "and that's something I never see anything written about. . . . It's always a trade-off and you're making a judgment call. And I'll be frank with you, you don't feel very comfortable. But you gotta do it."

————

PARLIAMENTARY VOTING RECORDS reveal that most MPs side with their parties on nearly every vote; but, in recalling their time in Ottawa, the MPs we interviewed wanted to make it clear that they had often felt heavily constrained. And most made a point of telling us about times when they didn't agree with their party, or had sought a concession such as permission to miss a vote in order to help manage their discomfort with the party line. In fact, almost all the recollections they volunteered were concerned with what it was like to be a member of a political party. And they weren't good. Time and time again, MPs told us how decisions made by party leadership seemed opaque, arbitrary and even juvenile, and how party demands inhibited their ability to serve their constituents.

The MPs' complaints raise an issue: Why join a political party? The difficulty, at least if one wants to be a successful parliamentarian, is that virtually every Canadian MP arrives under the banner of a political party. In the last thirty years, only two freshmen MPs have been elected as independents—Quebec City's André Arthur in the riding of Portneuf–Jacques-Cartier in 2006, and in 1984, Tony Roman in Toronto's York North. Even if there is little choice but to sign on with a party in order to get elected or to be effective in Parliament, belonging to a political party requires sacrifices from the MP. Part of that sacrifice is identity. Once an MP decides to run under a party banner, his or her identity becomes closely tied to the organization's brand and leader.

The inherent dichotomy in the role of an MP in a parliamentary democracy is clear—autonomy in the home riding; loyalty on Parliament Hill. "There may be some exceptions in those African dictatorships that are part of the Commonwealth and so on," said Leslie Seidle, research director of the Institute for Research on Public Policy, in an interview with the *Globe and Mail*. "But in the advanced parliamentary democracies, there is nowhere that has heavier, tighter party discipline than the Canadian House of Commons."

Later in the same article, University of Toronto professor Richard Simeon said much the same thing. "We are worse than the Australians, and much worse than the British, in terms of giving MPs the ability to act and to somehow make a difference," said Simeon. And of course, unlike our closest neighbour, the United States, Canada's tight party control has another aspect: the leaders of the party that controls the House of Commons also form the executive arm of government, thus furthering their power.

Dictating which way MPs vote is already imperious, but Canadian parties have long gone past that. These days, discipline is so tight that members must restrict their public comments to speaking points the party has provided. Party leaders enforce this discipline in order to be as certain as possible that legislation will pass. Dissent within a party could lead the media to criticize the party for poor organization. Such tight discipline also contributes to the public's ability to hold parties accountable at election time: if all members of a party vote in a particular way, then the party's positions are ostensibly clearer to the electorate.

The MPs we spoke with chafed against the party strictures, which all too often left them feeling uncomfortable and even hypocritical. As Liberal MP Sue Barnes put it, "I didn't leave my family and my city and a life to let somebody else tell me what to do, or to roll along with the flow." Conservative MP

Carol Skelton also vowed to speak up: "Going through the stage that I did in my life, in my thirties and forties and then when I reached my fifties, I really decided that if there's something that goes on that I don't want, I'm going to stand up and talk."

Conservative MP John Cummins responded to the advice of a friend in such situations. The friend reminded Cummins that one day he would no longer be an MP, and when that day came, he would have to look back and assess whether he had remained true to his own principles or the principles of his party: "At some point you are no longer going to be elected. You may be defeated or you may decide not to run again," Cummins said, summing up the friend's advice. "The only thing that is going to matter at that point is, how did I do the business when I was there? How did I conduct the people's business?" Cummins didn't want any regrets. "You want to have peace of mind when you're no longer there—you want to be able to look back and say, I stood up for the folks back home. . . . My view is, you represent the people first, the party second."

New Democrat MP Bill Blaikie's decision matrix on whether to vote with the party was less clearly defined. "Well," he said, "it's kind of a three-way thing between your constituents, your party and your conscience or your own judgment. But judgment and conscience aren't always the same thing, because not everything is a matter of conscience—because in order to operate within a political party, if everything is a matter of conscience, well then you are not going to be in a political party for long. . . . Not everything is a matter of conscience in the sense of, 'I have to resign,' or, 'I have to cast the dissenting vote,' in that sense of conscience. You express those differences of opinion and judgment within the caucus, and then one of the other principles of parliamentary life is that you abide by the majority decision unless you find it so troubling to your conscience . . . [or to your] sense of survival. [If] their party was asking them to take a position that was going to send them over the cliff, people have been known to cast the dissenting vote for that reason."

Discomfort with the extent of party discipline was expressed even by some Cabinet ministers. "I remember that there were bills when I was thinking, 'Why the heck am I standing up on that?' because I didn't necessarily believe [in the party's position]. But you're in the government, and you vote with your government," said former Liberal Cabinet minister Pierre Pettigrew.

The tension between party and politician is a natural and long-entrenched part of the parliamentary system. What we didn't expect to hear from the MPs during the exit interviews, however, was how poorly they felt the parties managed this tension, relying heavily on whipped votes, and punitive measures for those who did not fall in line.

Take the situation that faced the Progressive Conservative-turned-Liberal MP Bill Matthews in 2008, as the House of Commons considered extending Canada's military mission in Afghanistan. Matthews represented Random–Burin–St. George's in Newfoundland, and he displays the independent and pugnacious spirit that reflects the province's reputation. He also values consistency in his own voting record. He voted against renewing Canada's commitment to the Afghanistan mission when it came up in the legislature in 2006, as did sixty-six of his fellow Liberals. The matter came up again in the House two years later. This time, the debate concerned whether to extend the mission. "I was not in favour of the mission," Matthews said. "So why would I be in favour of extending it? That's the way I am, you see? . . . If I was against the mission two years ago, I am certainly against extending the mission now."

As the vote approached, staff from the whip's office approached Matthews to find out how he would vote. "Listen," Matthews said. "I voted against the mission. I'm not voting to extend the mission, so you know how I'm going to vote." He said he told them "a dozen times." And then, when it came time for him to actually vote in the House, he felt the eyes of the whip and the leader on him. "I stand up to vote against extending the mission," Matthews recounts. "And they're all looking at [me] like, 'What's wrong with him?'"

Matthews felt unjustly maligned by Liberal leader Stéphane Dion and his whip, Karen Redman. Several dozen other Liberals reversed their positions, but Matthews stood firm. "And *I'm* the bad guy?" Matthews said. "I am consistent. Those forty or so who are inconsistent, that's not me. Don't expect me to follow after the forty or so inconsistent ones. I'm not like that. . . . I've been against this from day one and I still am. . . . I'm not changing."

As with classroom seats in grade school, certain seating positions in the House of Commons are jealously coveted. The closer a seat is to the leader's seat at the front, the greater the status of the occupant. Soon after the Afghanistan vote, the party moved Matthews to a seat back by the rearmost curtain. "Punishment," Matthews observed. "They'd thought they'd penalize me by putting me back by the curtain. . . . That's Ottawa. That's some of the frustrating stuff about Ottawa—that's been frustrating over the years, in Ottawa—the dominance from the centre of whatever party it is that thinks it should control your everyday life."

Matthews found party control counterproductive to effective politics. "Because there's so many people—I've got to be careful what I say here—who are ambitious and eager to please and to do what they think is going to help them get ahead. And they put that before—and I've seen so much of that in both jurisdictions of public life—that people would sell their souls to have their chauffeur. And that's just . . . human nature, I suppose. Not *my* human nature, but for a lot of people it is: 'Whatever pleases the centre.' I could never be like that."

It's to be expected that the dozens of MPs elected to a single party will not agree on every issue; many of the former MPs we met with described episodes like Joe Comuzzi's. What we found surprising from the exit interviews was not only how often the MPs emphasized these disagreements, particularly since they voted nearly all the time with their parties, but also how their parties lacked a transparent and openly agreed-upon mechanism, beyond the confines of the committee or the caucus, for them to voice that dissent.

Ottawa convention has created what one could call a "ladder of dissent": a continuum of methods in which an MP may disagree with party policy, ranging from least public dissent to most. At the very least, an MP is able to disagree in private debate, in caucus, as long as he or she votes for the resultant legislation in the Commons. A second, and slightly more noticeable option, is to disagree privately and then abstain from the vote—an equivocal tactic that may allow one to save face with constituents while avoiding a loss of standing in the party. Finally, an MP can disagree by voting against the legislation in the House of Commons. This most public form of dissent is likely to summon some form of retribution from the party, as in the case of Bill Matthews.

The Reform Party featured some of the most hands-off approaches to party discipline in Canadian history, thanks to the fact that, according to its populist bent, it encouraged MPs to vote the way their constituents wished. Several MPs initially elected as members of the Reform Party also told us they were given guidelines on how to prioritize the factors informing their decisions about which way to vote. "The policy was loud and clear," said Reform-turned-Conservative MP Myron Thompson. "When it comes to vote, you vote the wishes of the people. If you can't determine what the wishes of the people are, then it was support the position of the party. And if the party didn't have a position on that, then and only then could you vote your own will, providing you could show that the will of the people [was] at loggerheads—50-50 type."

Thompson described the way Reform's policy toward dissent had changed once it transitioned into the Canadian Alliance and then the Conservative Party. "Caucus has agreed on this; this is the direction we are going to go. Maybe . . . 10 percent of you don't like this idea but you don't have a free vote on this. So we lost the free vote. You must follow the party policy—and I refused to.

"If I didn't like what we were doing, I would—and I talked to Preston Manning and even before I left I talked to Stephen Harper, and I said, 'I am going in there and I am not supporting your position. I am voting the will of my constituents. If I have to prove it to you, I can do that—but that's what

I am going to do.'" When the party asked, "Well, could you just not show up?" Thompson responded, "No. I *am* showing up. I am going in there and I am voting 'no.'"

Reform-turned-Conservative MP Paul Forseth, who left Parliament in 2006, described a similar shift in the party's receptivity to MP policy input, from the early days of Reform to the current iteration of the Conservative Party under Stephen Harper. Reform, Forseth said, encouraged a bottom-up policy that saw leader Preston Manning taking guidance from his MPs on how their constituents felt about an issue. In his experience, Forseth said, that approach fell by the wayside. "I don't think, even in our Conservative caucus [under Stephen Harper], that there is quite that emphasis anymore. It's more top-down driven. [In Reform] there was that emphasis on the fact that your membership in the caucus really made a difference, your voice was counted, and we would spend exhaustive times having individual members of the caucus come to the microphone to argue and debate."

Former NDP leader Ed Broadbent says he allowed the MPs under him to vote against the party in what he termed "exceptional cases." To qualify, the MP made the case for disagreement with the whole of the caucus—"if he could show it was not simply self-interest in preserving his or her seat but had good grounds for a policy difference from the party that was coherent with the interests in his or her community." After all, Broadbent points out, "We are all elected basically as members of parties."

Some conflict did happen under Broadbent—and when it did, he exerted himself to find a compromise. Take his experience with the one-time Saskatoon NDP MP Bob Ogle.

Like all NDPers, Ogle had been elected on a platform that was pro-choice. Problem was, Ogle was a Catholic priest who was strongly opposed to abortion. "So this was a matter of life or death philosophically," Broadbent said, speaking of the seriousness that Ogle felt about the issue. So when a vote came up in Parliament that hinged on personal principles about abortion, Broadbent lifted party discipline for Ogle, and Ogle alone. "I accepted his decision," Broadbent says, "even though he was elected by a program or party that accepted a woman's right to choose. It would be total hypocrisy on his part to vote, so he did not vote with the party on that instance—as I recall he abstained."

Chrétien-era Liberal whip Marlene Catterall downplayed concerns about the bonds of party discipline, at least as they existed in Jean Chrétien's government. Prior to her time in federal politics, she had been a municipal politician with the capacity to vote freely; she didn't have a party whip watching over her shoulder each time she cast a ballot. So before she made the decision to pursue a federal political office, she considered whether she wanted to subject herself to the behavioural restrictions required by party membership. "One of the things I really had to think about was, am I prepared to be part of a team and to have my freedom to speak out on issues . . . limited by being a representative of a party in the House of Commons?"

The way she reasoned, the party was a lot more important to voters than her individual name. "By a huge majority, people vote not for the Member of Parliament," Catterall said, mentioning the much-cited statistic that the candidate's name accounts for only 5 percent of the votes, with the party and leader accounting for the rest. "They vote for the party and the leader that they want governing the country. . . . How can a leader in the party . . . deliver on the commitments they made during the campaign unless people feel bound to defend those policies? You can't say I run for a party, I get elected because I am a representative of that party, but then once I get in Parliament I don't feel any obligations to what I said I was going to do once I went for election."

To enforce party discipline as whip, Catterall relied on informal processes. "If people really didn't want to go and vote," she said, "and I absolutely knew that it was something that was crucial to their constituency and that they weren't bullshitting me—if it really was something extremely important; they wanted to support the party but they just didn't feel they could vote for this, or they would be betraying the constituents—I would say, 'What do you want to do? Do you want to be sick? Do you want to go to a committee meeting somewhere out of town or to a conference out of the country?'"

After Chrétien resigned, Paul Martin brought in his own version of the ladder of dissent. The "three-line whip" was a discipline system that categorized bills in one of three ways. Liberal MP Roy Cullen contrasted Martin's comparatively lax party discipline with Chrétien's. "Under Mr. Chrétien everything seemed to be like a confidence vote," said Cullen. But Martin allowed more flexibility with his three-tier voting. "Tier one was like a confidence matter, such as a budget or Throne Speech [where MPs were expected to support the party]. Tier two would be policy matters that are very important and that MPs would be encouraged to support. Tier three was free votes. And if we thought that [an issue] was a category one instead of a category two, we could thrash that out beforehand," Cullen said.

Free votes, such as private members' business, were controversial, too. Even in this ostensibly independent arena, the MPs reported heavy party intervention. Bloc MP Odina Desrochers said that even when facing a free vote, his party still pressured MPs. "There are no real free votes. The political parties will say that it's a free vote to seem democratic, but if the leader has an opinion on it, he's going to put pressure on the membership so that you think like him," he said.

Bill Blaikie expressed frustration that the governing parties rarely adhered to allowing free votes once in power. "All these guys who said they were for free votes end up voting against private members' business because their government does not want it to happen," he said. MPs also expressed anxiety over potential reprisals from their peers over free votes. As Liberal-turned-Independent MP Pat O'Brien described it: "There are consequences for however you vote. There are free votes where you know that, while you're not going to get kicked out of the party, your name's now on somebody's hit list, or their 'do not promote' list."

If an MP did decide not to vote with his or her party, how could that dissent best be expressed? Was abstaining from a vote, for example, an honourable or cowardly form of dissent? On this question in particular there was much disagreement among our interviewed MPs. In 2002, when Liberal MP Stephen Owen held dual Cabinet roles of secretary of state for both Western economic diversification and for Indian affairs and northern development, he faced a vote about whether committee chairs should be elected or appointed. An enthusiastic adherent of all aspects of democracy, Owen believed committee chairs should be elected. The rest of the Cabinet disagreed. "I basically closed my briefing book and said to the prime minister, 'It's been an honour being in your Cabinet and I understand you need solidarity and so I have to resign.' So I left and I was caught up with two floors down at the front door by someone who ran after me and said, 'No, you have to come back.'"

Owen did go back. He and several close friends, also ministers, conferred in an anteroom to the Cabinet chamber, and they came up with a solution: Owen could abstain from the vote. "It was accepted that I wouldn't vote against the government, but I wouldn't vote at all," Owen said. "It allowed us to sort of say, okay, I accept the principle of Cabinet solidarity but the prime minister accepted that I could miss the vote." He synthesized what other MPs had also described: "There is a whole range of ways you can [signal] dissent and sometimes you can do it tactfully, strategically, and sometimes you can just make a fool of yourself or seem disloyal and disrespectful. So I think you have to be very careful. There is an expectation. You join the party because you believe in the full package and on so many issues it is necessary to act collectively—so you can't just be a maverick—but there are going to be [times] too that you have to be willing to debate your point within caucus, or Cabinet, as strenuously as you can and then accept the will of the majority, the consensus, or step aside. . . . But then there will be lines that you won't cross."

Others felt that, as a mechanism for disagreement, abstention was cowardly. "You're sent here to do a job," said Liberal MP Paul DeVillers. "Do it. Don't hide in the washroom when it's time to take that stand." DeVillers was among the former MPs who expressed frustration with members who voted against their party. He—and many others—framed party discipline in terms of being a "team player." Said DeVillers, "It annoyed me when people would vote against the party with no consequence. As a team player, that annoyed me. If I was only in it for myself, I'd be voting here and voting there."

Perhaps Russ Powers was one of the MPs who annoyed DeVillers. They were in the Liberal caucus at the same time, yet Powers was at the other end of the spectrum in considering how to signal dissent. Powers acknowledged that, while he and his colleagues were there to pass legislation in the best interests of the country, they were also required to develop policy that benefited the party's prospects for re-election. "You had to adhere to the policy or [face] the wrath of the whip," Powers explained: "Now, I can tell you that over the nineteen months I was there I probably voted against my party six times, but I was able to explain the rationale and I was never castigated or hung out. . . . I supported pieces of legislation the Conservatives introduced. The perfect [example] is the gun legislation: I come from an urban riding that is part of an old city, which has mafia connections and gang crime, and their proposal for punishment for the use of handguns made sense from a political standpoint and it made sense from a practical standpoint. . . . Some nice pieces of legislation came out of the NDP and some nice pieces of legislation came out of the Bloc Québécois—as long as the Bloc was not self-serving from the standpoint of [being] Quebec-centric; a lot of their stuff was really beneficial."

Bloc MP Stéphane Bergeron described how he handled a situation in which a high-profile economic announcement ran counter to the interests of his riding. "I was torn between the need to work for the well-being of my constituents, and my personal values that led me to want to defend the position of my colleagues. I discussed my dilemma with my party leader, who accepted that I could deviate from the party line by not taking part in the debate or the vote." He left the discussion, he said, satisfied that he could take the values of his party into account without working against his constituents' interests.

Among our interview subjects, the MPs who had been in leadership roles tended to be more sanguine about subsuming individual opinion under the party umbrella. It's no surprise that people closer to power or who exert direct control over many of the decisions prefer the system as it is, even if those further from the top are less satisfied. Consider NDP leader Ed Broadbent, who led his party for fourteen years: "Ultimately, the MP has to decide what is the right thing to do, and to some real extent it should be to the party he's campaigned on because . . . overwhelmingly the evidence is [that people] vote for you because you are a member of a certain party. So they expect when they're voting that, when you get to the House of Commons, you're going to promote that [party's] agenda and whether it's a Conservative, Liberal or NDP agenda, I think that's a primary obligation of an MP."

Or take Bill Graham, the Liberal MP who acted as interim leader for his party after Paul Martin stepped down following the 2006 election. Adhering to party discipline, Graham said, "is the nature of the bargain we made when we ran as Liberal[s]. . . . I was not elected to be Bill Graham—it's not the U.S. Congress; I was elected under Mr. Chrétien on a Liberal Party platform. . . . In order to deliver I have to vote with my party. My constituents would come in to me and say, 'We don't want you to vote for that'—even though it's party policy. I would say, 'I am sorry. The nature of the democratic government in which we live requires me to support my government.'"

Paul Martin also accepted that there was no way around this occasional discomfort: "You have just got to make it work. I mean, there are going to be areas where you disagree with your party, and you disagree; but there are going to be areas where the disagreement that you have is not crucial and if that's the case then go on with your party, because fundamentally the party got you elected, not you. Unless you put a little bit of water in your wine and your colleagues do the same thing, then you may win minor victories but you will lose the big battle and you don't want to do that."

THE RELATIONSHIP BETWEEN an MP and his or her political party is much like that between the local owner of a national restaurant franchise and its corporate management—an observation captured by UBC professor R. Kenneth Carty in describing the "franchise bargain" of Canadian politics. Prospective franchisees acquire the benefits of affiliation with the larger brand and are given an opportunity to bring ideas forward that, if accepted and rolled out, can benefit the wider company. Yet the local entrepreneurs must meet the conditions the central franchise office sets in order to be allowed to operate a new location—pay a flat fee up front, plus a percentage of royalties on sales, for instance. Then, while actually operating, the franchisee must follow a set of stringent regulations mandated by head office, including the appearance and content of posted menus, branding, interior design and employee processes. These regulations can cause friction between a franchisee and the parent company—but typically, franchisees submit to the regulations because their business is so much more valuable when it carries the national brand.

Consider the business of poutine, the popular Québécois fast-food dish that traditionally involves slathering french fries with layers of cheese curds and steaming hot gravy. In 2010 Canadians consumed about 78.4 million servings of the stuff. Although its exact origin is disputed, consensus holds that it was invented in a small town east of Montreal in the mid-1950s. Its popularity spread throughout the region and eventually the province, and today poutine is typically served by burger outlets or the sort of all-night diners frequented by study-weary and party-famished students. In 1989, at the suggestion of an Ottawa franchisee, the Canadian-owned french fry company New York Fries experimented with the dish. Like many franchise businesses, New York Fries is organized with centralized management and a network of locally owned businesses that follow a set of corporate operating principles. Based on the success of his company's initial foray into poutine, owner Jay Gould has made the menu item a staple at all its one hundred and twenty Canadian locations. Poutine is big business for New York Fries; by 2008 it accounted for more than half the company's revenue.

Just as New York Fries' head office defines and circumscribes much of the daily life of a local franchisee, MPs—whether on the backbench or in a leadership position—understand that their relationship with their party defines their lives as parliamentarians. New York Fries' foray into poutine shows what can happen when a national office listens to its local members, and how an individual in a large, rigid organization can actively contribute ideas that lead to wider growth. In theory, little prevents similar outcomes from happening in politics, but many of the MPs we interviewed did not describe their experiences this way. A major difference, of course, between political parties and MPs, and New York Fries and its franchisees, is that the poutine merchants have established business practices and management tactics to facilitate such brainstorming and to mitigate the tensions that invariably occur when balancing local and companywide objectives. Judging from what former MPs said during our interviews, few political parties have even heard of management theory—let alone learned how they can exploit the front-line insight of the franchisee to strengthen the brand as a whole.

For example, the ex-MPs we met with routinely expressed frustration with their party's inscrutable manipulation of what, in a business, would be called human resources. Parties made seemingly arbitrary decisions about advancement and discipline within their ranks. What sort of performance was valued? What actions would be punished? We've already noted the absence of any formal job description for an MP. Nor did we come across any sort of systematic method that party leadership used to evaluate MPs' work. With the exception of the occasional—albeit important—mandate letters delivered to Cabinet ministers outlining the prime minister's expectations, Canadian federal political parties set few goals for their MPs beyond winning elections. Nor do they deliver constructive feedback in any systematic way between elections.

As a result, the only guidelines for performance—at least as the MPs often described them—came in the form of ad hoc and seemingly arbitrary decisions about advancement and demotion. The MPs to whom we spoke expressed confusion as to how they were evaluated by their party leadership, and how promotions or discipline were allocated. They had a general sense: making it into Cabinet meant they were doing something right; being banished to the back row of the House of Commons meant they were doing something wrong. But reasons for these decisions were seldom given.

Cabinet posts were particularly controversial. Most MPs acknowledged the importance of balance in gender, region and ethnicity in promotion decisions. But several said that too many appointments were undeserved—or allotted for inscrutable or unknown reasons. Several MPs suggested that a promotion was more often tied to their demographic profile or the riding they represented—or to their ability to fundraise for the party—rather than to how well they'd done their job.

Even those who were promoted sometimes expressed surprise at their promotions, particularly when the appointments had little to do with their pre-parliamentary knowledge or interests. Eleni Bakopanos recounted receiving a call from the PMO, informing her that she'd received an appointment in the justice ministry. She thought there'd been a mistake. "I said, 'Tell the prime minister to call me back—I didn't finish law school.'"

"When I was appointed to Cabinet [as the secretary of state for physical activity and sport], sports came as a complete surprise. I didn't see it coming," said Liberal MP Paul DeVillers, adding that he had no background in the area, save for running in his spare time.

"What was the most frustrating was to see people recognized and rewarded that you know are less competent than other people, because of political debts," said Liberal MP

Marlene Catterall. "You like to think that when you work hard and make an important contribution it's going to be recognized and appreciated, and that doesn't always happen. That's one of the most disappointing things about politics."

The MPs told us that other rewards were also distributed in an equally confusing manner, and at the party's whim. For example, permission to travel for parliamentary business—an important aspect of committee work—is granted by the party whip. But as Bill Matthews described it, if you weren't "playing the game," your travel request would be denied. "You can see who was going where. All you had to do was reflect on a six-month period and see who was rewarded and penalized," Matthews said.

FEW PEOPLE TODAY recognize how haphazard the evolution of political parties in Canada has been. As informal gatherings of federal politicians, they date back to Confederation; Canada's first federal election saw Sir John A. Macdonald's Liberal-Conservative Party beat the Liberal Party. But parties themselves were only recognized in limited ways and weren't even mentioned on the ballot until a 1970 change to the Canada Elections Act. In addition to providing voters with greater clarity, this change was designed to ensure clearer accountability for the ways in which political parties spent public monies.

Increasingly, laws were established to clarify parties' financial obligations. The 1974 Elections Expenses Act, for instance, required parties to conform to spending limits and public disclosure regulations in order to receive federal funding. And some of that funding came in the form of tax credits designed to encourage individuals rather than corporations or unions to contribute to parties—a measure later stepped up to create an outright ban on corporate and union donations.

Legislation in 2004 further institutionalized the place of parties by instituting government subsidies to parties through a quarterly allowance tied to the number of votes the party received in the previous election. (This is the subsidy that the Harper government tried to eliminate during one of its minority governments, and eventually did vote to phase out later when it had a majority.) Finally, another significant public subsidy comes in the form of election rebates, in which the government reimburses half of the national campaign expense to any registered party that receives at least 2 percent of the national popular vote.

Through tax subsidies, donations and the quarterly allowance, parties are government-funded to the tune of almost two-thirds of their annual budgets. In exchange, parties are required to report certain aspects of their operations: the number of campaign contributions, their size and, if the contribution is over $200, the name of the contributor. They are required to submit a statement of assets and liabilities to the government, and they must be audited.

However, the reporting that parties are required to do, and the overall extent of their regulation, is less than what is required of Canadian charities, and far less than what is required of publicly traded Canadian corporations. This, in spite of the fact that parties receive proportionally more public subsidies than either charities or corporations. Parties also have remarkable power over the lives of ordinary Canadians; certainly more power than most charities or corporations. Given this, why are we hearing descriptions of management and human resources practices that appear, to those involved, as disorganized as something out of a university student club? Today's parties concentrate their power in the office of the party leader and its unelected professional staff, many of whom are themselves not long out of university. The MPs described the nomination process as a perplexing and bewildering process with little consistency across ridings and noted the absence of an orientation process for rookie MPs, either from Parliament or their parties. They dictate what the MPs say in the House and increasingly in committees. They draw on Canadians to join and contribute to their coffers, with little opportunities for meaningful contributions beyond that. What do MPs and citizens get in return?

At the dawn of the millennium, political scientists William Cross and Lisa Young conducted a survey of members from each of Canada's major political parties—3,872 members who, because the survey occurred between elections, tended to be long-term, active party stalwarts. Their survey found that party members "were not satisfied with their ability to shape party policy and . . . particularly resentful of the extent to which political professionals have usurped the role of the party member."

Although parties do not regularly report official membership numbers, Cross and Young estimated that between 1 and 2 percent of Canadians belong to a political party at any one time—a statistic, they said, that ranks us at the bottom of Western democracies. Why are so few Canadians joining parties? Cross and Young believe it's because "voters do not see membership in political parties as a way of influencing the country's politics." "Even the parties' core group of consistent members," they say, "are largely dissatisfied with the role they play in ongoing party decision-making. . . . The evidence is clear that voters do not see participation in parties as an effective way of influencing public policy. Rather, they prefer activism in interest and advocacy groups, leaving the parties with an aging and often dispirited membership." There is no indication that anything has changed in the ensuing dozen years. If anything, the problem has grown worse.

Political parties are critical parts of Canada's democratic infrastructure and serve at least four important functions: engaging citizens in politics, selecting candidates for elected office, developing and aggregating policy perspectives and contesting elections. But as the MPs tell it, except for contesting elections the parties do few of these things very well. If Canada's political parties were corporations, they'd collapse under the weight of their own mismanagement. In fact, parties amplified these frustrations by providing their MPs with little guidance or structure, and by intervening arbitrarily—often without explanation—in the MPs' work. The end effect? Even MPs felt alienated from their parties.

Democracy relies on citizen engagement to thrive—at the very least, it needs citizens to vote. If they don't, political leaders lack the legitimacy required to rule. Which leads us to the following question: If MPs are disenchanted with their own parties, then how can we expect regular citizens to engage with those same parties at all? MPs probably benefit more than anyone from party membership. And if they claim the party leadership pushes them away from constructive politics, is it any wonder that so many Canadians can't even be bothered to cast a vote?

"Canadians believe they need political parties, but they do not like or trust them," says Kenneth Carty. He believes that Canadian federal politics is populated by "leader-centred, leader-dominated parties" that allow little room for "individual partisans to do much more than show up at the polls on election day." Nor does the system provide much satisfaction for many MPs, he observes. Once the MPs head off to Ottawa, "they come under the sway of the leadership and take their voting instructions from the parliamentary top of the party, not the grassroots bottom." This leads to one of the system's defining tensions: "This separation between the opportunities for citizen participation and the practices of institutional representation proves, ultimately, to be an unsatisfactory way to engage in democratic politics." Carty points to the unfortunate results: "Some MPs simply leave . . . and some voters abandon the parties."

Carty corroborates the implications of the situation the MPs described to us: the parties are at least partially responsible for creating a disenfranchised electorate. Canadian political parties, he says, are "the underdeveloped institutions of a political elite playing a highly personalized game of electoral politics: they are not the instruments of an engaged or even interested citizenry." And that, Carty says, "shrinks the prospect that the party system might be seen as an effective agency through which citizens might hope to make a contribution to the public life of their society. . . . The stark reality is that most Canadians no longer like, trust or join national political parties; they do not believe the party system offers them a tool for choosing or influencing their national government." Add this to the composite picture that our MPs painted of a feckless, even negligent, attitude on the part of the party leadership toward the party's most important human resources, the MPs themselves, and you have a recipe for undermining the democratic process in the House of Commons and in Canada as a whole today.

NOW LET'S FINISH the story of Joe Comuzzi. Once he had voted against his party on gay marriage, Comuzzi found it difficult to return to his previous role as a good soldier. Coming off a narrow 2006 federal election win by only 403 votes against a strong NDP competitor, and after a transition from government to opposition for the Liberal Party as well as a transition in Liberal leadership from Comuzzi's long-time friend Paul Martin to Stéphane Dion, Comuzzi again voted against his party in September 2006, this time on softwood lumber legislation. Then in March 2007 Comuzzi did something that was anathema to a member of the Liberal Party caucus: he indicated to Liberal leader Stéphane Dion that he intended to support the Conservative government's budget bill. The bill included millions of dollars in research funding that Comuzzi believed would allow a molecular medicine research centre to be built in his Thunder Bay riding, creating three hundred new jobs. "To vote against it, every citizen in Thunder Bay would be tremendously upset with me," Comuzzi said on *Mike Duffy Live*.

Dion subsequently forced Comuzzi, by then a nineteen-year party veteran, out of the Liberal caucus. "This is not a happy day," Comuzzi told the *Globe and Mail*, saying that he expected his seat in the House of Commons to move to "someplace where you get a nosebleed." He joined Stephen Harper's Conservative Party that June. "This is not an easy decision,"

Comuzzi said before a crowd of Thunder Bay supporters. "You can't be a member of one group and all of a sudden change. . . . [But] I found myself increasingly at odds with some of the Liberal Party on a variety of issues." Later, Comuzzi indicated that he would not seek re-election after the conclusion of the 39th Parliament, which ended its session on September 7, 2008. He had been the MP for Thunder Bay–Superior North for twenty years.

CHAPTER EIGHT

Colluding in Their Servitude

W e have heard examples of what can happen when an individual MP disagrees with the party line. But what about challenges posed by MPs' relationship to the party leader? And, more to the point, what are the mechanisms of the leader's relationship to the party as a whole? What happens when the leader loses the support of many MPs?

That's what occurred in the spring of 2001, when a group of Canadian Alliance MPs stood in a line before the assembled Ottawa media, cameras flashing. There were eight of them that day: Art Hanger, Chuck Strahl, Gary Lunn, Val Meredith, Jim Gouk, Jim Pankiw, Grant McNally and Jay Hill. They were doing something highly unusual in Canadian politics. The MPs were in the process of proclaiming publicly that they wanted their party leader to step down.

Their leader was Stockwell Day, heading into the final months of his first year at the head of the newly formed Canadian Alliance party. He'd won the leadership in July 2000 with 63 percent of the vote, defeating the founder of the Alliance's precursor Reform Party, Preston Manning. But Day's missteps had begun with his first press conference after being elected to the House of Commons in a by-election for the B.C. riding of Okanagan–Coquihalla. The setting was a beach on the shores of Okanagan Lake, and Day arrived from the water, zooming toward the lectern on a Jet Ski. He stood before the microphones in a wetsuit. As an entrance orchestrated to create a first impression, it was seen as contrived, perhaps a little flashy, and would come to be perceived as Day's first error of judgment in a list that would soon grow long.

But what *really* triggered the erosion of Day's support was his performance in his first federal election as leader, in November 2000. The strategy behind Reform's rebranding into the Canadian Alliance involved a play for electoral relevance east of the Ontario-Manitoba border. It was an attempt to transform the party's brand from a populist Western protest party into one driven by broad-based national conservatism. Day's election took place because his comparative youth and athleticism were expected to better appeal to voters in Ontario and Eastern Canada. But support for the former Alberta MLA wavered in caucus after the public revelation that settling a defamation lawsuit against Day had cost the Alberta provincial government almost $800,000. Then came the news that two of his supporter MPs had hired an undercover investigator to look into the affairs of Prime Minister Jean Chrétien. The Alliance's first federal election took place on November 27, 2000. Up against Jean Chrétien's Liberals, Day's Alliance won only 66 seats compared to the Liberals' majority win of 172; the nation's other candidate to become the national conservative party, Joe Clark's Progressive Conservatives, won 12. The 66 seats were enough to make the Alliance the Official Opposition, but the result under Day was far short of what many Alliance members had hoped.

Once the dust settled, rumblings of insurrection escaped Day's caucus. To calm the dissent, Day called a caucus meeting on May 2, 2001. It ended up lasting four hours, and it didn't work. "I think for the good of the party, Mr. Day should step down," said MP Art Hanger, then a Canadian Alliance MP representing the Alberta riding of Calgary Northeast, who had first been elected for Reform in 1993. "My views as I've expressed are not just *my* views. They go far beyond me."

It soon became apparent that some, and perhaps many, of the Alliance MPs agreed with Hanger. "What was not known publicly was that it was a very large number of us behind closed doors in the caucus—in fact, I would say 90 percent of the caucus—wanted our leader to resign," Jay Hill said in his exit interview. "Finally it got untenable and those of us who were very close to the epicentre of the problems came to the realization we could no longer look [at] ourselves in the mirror. And it's very difficult to shave in the morning if you can't stand to look at yourself."

As May progressed, more MPs went public with their doubts about Day. "I am not prepared to pretend that I have confidence in the leadership," said Alliance MP Val Meredith. She criticized Stockwell Day for his "lack of judgment and a certain degree of dishonesty coming out of the leadership office." And then came Jim Gouk: "I cannot in good conscience continue to support Stockwell Day."

On May 15, 2001 the dissenting MPs held a news conference to publicize their insurrection. Acting as the contingent's spokesperson was former Alliance Government House Leader Chuck Strahl. "We realize that by speaking out there are implications, including the fact that we will be suspended from caucus," Strahl said. "But we are convinced that over the past few months the current leadership has exercised consistently bad judgment, dishonest communications and lack of fidelity to our party's policies. Since we do not wish to be associated with such practices, we have chosen to speak out today in an effort to bring about change.

"Some will argue that we should just be quiet," Strahl said. "But it is simply not acceptable for women and men of principle to stand by while the hopes and dreams of our own members and the strong desire of our voters for a positive conservative alternative to the Liberals [are] put at risk." And: "When loyalty to the leader comes up against loyalty to the principles and policies upon which we were elected, then the decision we make is neither difficult nor optional. You do what is right. You speak out. And you ask others to consider doing the same."

The dissidents triggered a nationwide conversation on the nature of political loyalty. Such a public revolt against party leadership by a block of sitting MPs was nearly unprecedented in contemporary Canadian politics. Should the MPs have kept their rebellion private, as an in-caucus affair?

So, what does happen when the party leader loses the confidence of the MPs he or she leads? The answer, in Canadian politics, is that in most cases MPs do nothing—or at least, nothing that we, the public, can see. Which begs a question: Why is insurrection so rare in the modern era of Canadian politics? Other parliamentary democracies feature a much more delicate balance of power between caucus and leaders. There are revolts; there are mutinies. In November 1990, in the wake of an unpopular poll tax in the UK, for instance, one such insurrection concluded the leadership of no less a figure than Prime Minister Margaret Thatcher, a veteran of eleven years running her country and three election wins. Similarly, Australian prime minister Kevin Rudd resigned in 2010 when his deputy prime minister, Julia Gillard, executed a coup within Labour Party ranks. Rudd returned the favour, toppling Gillard in June 2013, only to find his party defeated in a general election a few months later.

Why doesn't this sort of thing happen in Canada? Part of it is structural: unlike the case in Britain or Australia, Canadian party leaders are chosen by the wider party membership, not by MPs directly. But it's also a reflection of a parliamentary culture that prizes stability. Even with the extreme levels of dissent in the Alliance case, some—and perhaps most—MPs perceived that it was best to do nothing. To keep quiet.

What came through in our interviews with Strahl, Solberg, Hill and Hanger was how painful it was for them to come out publicly with their disagreement with their party leader. Hanger, a former crime scenes investigator on the homicide beat of the Calgary Police Service, a tough guy not averse to conflict, called it the most difficult day of his political career. "I found no satisfaction in that," Hanger said. "That was a tough time."

"I will always defend what we did," said Jay Hill. "I believe it was done with the strongest of principles and integrity. It was extremely difficult. I don't know whether I would do it again, what we went through and we put our party through and our colleagues and our supporters back home—all that angst and stress and pressure—and our families. I think probably if I had to do it over again I would just quit."

It's a remarkable statement. Jay Hill and his fellow MPs displayed courage. Their actions helped trigger a situation that led to the uniting of the country's conservative movement, which in turn led to the electoral successes of the Conservative Party of Canada. So why the regret?

CANADIAN PARTY LEADERS today enjoy a remarkable amount of power when measured against their peers in Canadian history, or against leaders in similar parliamentary systems around the world. Consider the prime minister. In 2007 the Irish political scientist Eoin O'Malley evaluated twenty-two of the world's parliamentary democracies in the context of "prime ministerial influence on policy" through the lens of an expert survey. In such countries as the UK, New Zealand, Israel, Australia and Canada, the survey asked between fifteen and twenty political scientists per country to rate, on a scale from one to nine, the extent to which prime ministers who held the office in the previous twenty years were able to influence policy output. The result? Canadian prime ministers ranked as the most powerful.

The Canadian prime minister did not always exercise such authority. Sir John A. Macdonald behaved more like a first among equals. The responsibilities of his office were such that he didn't require an office secretary, never mind a hired team of political advisors. In addition, Canada's first prime minister had to struggle with "loose fish" MPs who wished to stay independent of any political party. During Macdonald's five-year first term, fellow Tory MPs voted against the Macdonald government's wishes eighteen times. Macdonald survived and, Canada survived, arguably because the restrictions of party discipline weren't so tight 150 years ago. (Historians might note that Macdonald's superior use of patronage certainly helped him too.)

Some pundits regard the 1919 Liberal Party convention, which saw William Lyon Mackenzie King elected leader, as the beginning of the transfer of power from individual MPs to the head of their party. Before that convention, the parliamentary caucus of Liberal MPs elected the leader. At the 1919 convention, it was the party members in attendance as delegates who elected the leader. This change was designed to encourage greater participation in politics on the part of the party membership and ushered in a dramatic change in a leader's accountability. King's predecessor as Liberal leader, Sir Wilfrid Laurier, had been accountable to his MPs, and required their trust and approval to govern. King, elected by the will of a larger sample of party members, was accountable not to the MPs but rather to a hazier and less well-defined group, the party at large. The effect was a decrease in the leader's accountability and a corresponding increase in the leader's power.

But it was during the Pierre Trudeau years, scholars and pundits say, that power really surged toward the PMO, thanks to a number of steps, some planned, some unintended. Trudeau had served in predecessor Lester B. Pearson's Cabinet as both justice minister and parliamentary secretary to the prime minister. He found the power structure too flat, and thought the system lacked discipline. So when he assumed the leadership he moved to consolidate the power of the PMO by expanding it and by holding more frequent Cabinet meetings. "Pierre Trudeau and his key advisors are generally held responsible for inaugurating the ever-expanding and centralizing power of the PMO," according to historian Allan Levine. "The change was inevitable. In the late sixties, government in Canada got bigger and more bureaucratic, and some semblance of order and efficiency had to be maintained."

The most recent legislative change in this direction came in the 1970 Election Act amendments, which added the requirement that the party leader approve of each candidate running for the party, previously the job of the local constituency association that organized and oversaw the nomination race. From that day forward, the party leader had the prerogative, albeit rarely exercised, to refuse to sign nomination papers, even if that candidate won the local nomination race. The new regulation changed the power dynamics inherent in an MP's job. Even if rarely acted on, the threat of unsigned nomination papers suddenly hung over MPs' heads and made them think twice about speaking out. MPs had until then been accountable to their constituents; from that point on they were accountable also to the party, and to the leader specifically.

Another change that brought power to the leader's office happened in the early '80s, again under Trudeau, when Liberal MP Jeanne Sauvé was Speaker of the House. As a time-saving measure, Sauvé asked the parties to begin providing in advance the names of MPs who would be standing up to speak in the Members' Statements. On the face of it, this seemed a purely administrative request. Rather than Sauvé having to solicit the names of MPs who wished to address the House during the Members' Statements, the responsibility would now fall to the party, which presumably had a better sense of who wished to speak and when. But in practical terms, the step handed additional power to the party apparatus. It gave the leader's office de facto approval over whether and which individual MPs could issue Members' Statements.

Each successive majority PM has continued Trudeau's trend of consolidating power in the PMO. Brian Mulroney was considered a master at keeping his caucus too busy and too buttered up to engage in the petty machinations that might otherwise have sapped his power. Jean Chrétien—whose leadership long-time political columnist Jeffrey Simpson characterized in the title of his book *The Friendly Dictatorship*—perpetuated the trend. For example, Chrétien, under deadline from the Americans, opted not to call Parliament back into session before committing Canadian troops in the wake of the September 11, 2001, attacks on the World Trade Center. Journalists and academics have noted, both during and after Chrétien's time in office, many instances in which policy and spending decisions were made without Cabinet consultation. As one of Chrétien's senior policy advisors wrote in his memoirs, decisions were "made solely by the prime minister and the minister of finance, rather than by the whole Cabinet."

"Our concentration of power is greater than in any other government with a federal Cabinet system," said Gordon Robertson, former clerk of the Privy Council, the professionally staffed body of public servants whose role it is to advise the prime minister on important matters. "With the lack of checks and balances, the prime minister in Canada is perhaps the most unchecked head of government among the democracies."

When Chrétien was criticized for his autocratic methods, the political observers around him guessed that he would represent the apex of the power that accrued to the PMO. "Mr. Savoie and Mr. Robertson believe the centralization of power in the PMO has gone as far as it can go," concluded one newspaper story from 2002 on the topic of prime-ministerial power. And, for a time, Chrétien's successor, Paul Martin, did ease the hammerlock from his MPs' necks with his six-point plan to correct what he called Parliament's "democratic deficit," including the three-line whipping that eased party discipline in the House of Commons.

But the accrual of executive power continued under Martin's Conservative successor, Stephen Harper. Some MPs who served under Harper portrayed him as someone who occasionally eased the bonds of party discipline, at least while he was in opposition. Jim Gouk recalled Harper being flexible. "If there was a piece of legislation, I went to Stephen and I would say, 'I've got a serious problem with this,' and I'd explain why and he [would say], 'Okay, I understand that. You know, you are going to have to look to your conscience on this. There will be no repercussions [if you] vote the other way.'"

Nevertheless, Harper displayed autocratic tendencies even as the prime minister of a minority government. During his first year as prime minister he presented a motion recognizing Quebec as a "nation" inside a united Canada. The motion passed 266 to 16. But he had presented the motion without first consulting Michael Chong, his minister of intergovernmental affairs. Chong resigned from Cabinet in protest. In the wake of the October 2008 federal election that left Harper's Conservatives 12 seats shy of a majority government, the Conservatives' post-election economic update included two major acts of policy. The first would end the per-vote public subsidies that required the federal government to provide political parties with funding based on the number of election votes received—a measure instituted by Jean Chrétien's Liberal government in 2004. The second would ban strikes by public service unions.

What emerged in the wake of the update was the extent to which these measures had been unilateral decisions made by Harper himself, without the support of caucus. Neither measure had been discussed at a recent Conservative policy convention. Columnist Jeffrey Simpson suggested the policy measures were mistakes that stemmed from the autocratic nature of PMO policy making. "Mr. Harper makes decisions himself, or in an exceptionally closed circle. When his worst instincts are on the loose, there are inadequate checks in the system he has created around him, and few people willing or able to curb those instincts," Simpson wrote.

"That's why at the very last minute, the Prime Minister's Office sent over to the Finance Department those political zingers to include in the statement, without ministers or deputies knowing. And that procedure illustrates wider truths about this government: the centralization of power in Mr. Harper's hands, his office's fundamental distrust of most ministers and their staffs, and the Prime Minister's insistence that politics should drive decisions."

Harper eventually prorogued Parliament to avoid an early December 2008 non-confidence vote, and when MPs returned nearly two months later in January, the legislation was off the table. Ottawa observers interpreted the episode as a reflection on the limits of prime-ministerial power. But Harper's gambit backfired only because he had a minority government. Had he enjoyed the majority he's had since the 2011 election, the legislation almost certainly would have passed.

"Prime ministers currently dominate the machinery of government to an extent that was not possible forty years ago," writes Donald Savoie, one of the country's leading academics studying Parliament. Many have outlined the vast number of ways the prime minister is able to exercise power in Ottawa. The PM can exert influence over thousands of appointments, committee positions and plum Cabinet posts. And as leader of the party, the prime minister exercises a tremendous amount of control over the MPs in Parliament, dictating how they vote, when they speak in Parliament, and what they say when they do stand up to speak—as well as any number of other potential levers of coercion. "In short, the prime minister is head of government with limited checks on his or her power inside government or in Parliament if the PM's party holds a majority of seats," writes Savoie.

Fast-forward nearly five years to a majority Harper government. Now enjoying virtually unchecked power to enact legislative measures, Harper ended up scrapping the per-vote public party subsidy. He's also exercised his power over occasionally rebellious MPs. Take Conservative backbencher MP Mark Warawa's private member's motion to condemn sex-selective abortion. The Warawa motion contradicted Prime Minister Harper's campaign promise to avoid bringing up the matter of abortion during his term in government. In March 2013, the multipartisan subcommittee of MPs that oversees private members' business prevented Warawa from putting forward the motion, so he attempted to address the issue as a one-minute Members' Statement— but party leadership once again prevented him from addressing the House.

Harper's moves to silence Warawa attracted censure from the press and other MPs, even in his own caucus, who regarded the matter as an issue of free speech as well as MP agency. The Warawa affair became a symbol of the extent that party leadership controlled its Members of Parliament. Warawa was avowedly pro-life. Many of the people who protested his silencing were avowedly pro-choice, but nonetheless defended the British Columbia MP's attempt to put forward the motion. "This isn't a team," observed Andrew Coyne in the *National Post*, with the Conservative Party of Canada in mind. "It's a mob: mindless, frightened, without purpose or direction except what the leader decides, and unquestioning in its acceptance of whatever the leader decrees. . . . This is what has become of MPs, then—the people we elect to represent us, the ones who are supposed to give voice to our beliefs and stand up for our interests. They may not vote, in the vast majority of cases, except as the leader tells them. They may no longer, as of this week, bring private member's bills or motions, except those the leader accepts. They may not even speak in the House, unless the leader allows." The House of Commons speaker Andrew Scheer later ruled that nothing prevented MPs from standing to be recognized, bringing home the difference between the rules and their application in a party-dominated Parliament.

All of this is to the detriment of anyone who might look to Ottawa to see how our national affairs play out. Long gone are the days when Question Period involved a genuine exchange of questions and answers. Today, as any observer will tell you, it's forty-five minutes of political marketing. Private members' business, where individual MPs were once free to vote as they wished, is now increasingly used by all parties to test prospective legislation. All that remains free of party scripting is a small sliver of time during Members' Statements—fifteen minutes in each parliamentary day for MPs to speak in the House on items they deem of interest to their constituents or to themselves. And if present trends continue, this too may soon be gone.

WHY HAVE MPs allowed their power to be siphoned away as they have? Why don't MPs exercise the remaining freedom they still possess? Why don't they shrug off the shackles of the leadership? According to former Conservative MP Inky Mark, there's one very good reason: "They're scared—they're scared of the leader, scared of the caucus officers," he said, referring to the MPs in party leadership positions, such as the whip. "They are scared; they are just bullied. . . . Do you know what they're afraid of? They are afraid of not climbing the ladder. They are afraid of not getting the plum jobs."

"One of the things that has concerned me over my time in Ottawa is the powers that the party leaders have taken in respect of candidates," said Peter Milliken, former Liberal MP for Kingston and the Islands and Speaker of the House for a decade. In our interview with him, Milliken made some direct and striking comments about the ways political parties have drifted in recent years. He mentioned the fact that policy conventions aren't as substantive as they used to be. He mentioned the stipulation that required candidates for political office to have the approval of their party leader. "So if the leader does not like the candidate, he says I am not signing this certificate," Milliken says. "In my view, that is completely contrary to a system of democratic representation, where it's the constituency that chooses the candidate, not the leader. And we have moved away from that. Some of the party constitutions allow the leader to appoint [candidates]. I think that is wrong. If anybody should do the appointment it should be the riding president, who is elected by the riding association. But they do not want to do that anymore, and I just find that offensive and contrary to a parliamentary democracy."

MPs' irrelevance to the election of political leaders also troubled Milliken, referring to the Liberal Party's move to make the leadership vote far more populist by extending eligibility to vote, not simply to convention delegates but to any valid party member registered to vote (Milliken's interview took place before the creation of the Liberals' "supporter" category, which expands the pool of those eligible to vote for the leader even further).

For his part, Milliken believes the caucus should choose the party leader. "This is a parliamentary democracy," says the former Speaker. "The leader shouldn't be imposed by a vote now of all the party members across the country. The caucus should have a veto on that choice, in my view, if we are going to have a properly functioning parliamentary democracy. The Members of Parliament are the ones who ought to be choosing the person who is going to be their spokesperson or leader or whatever, in the Chamber, not some outside forces who elect somebody who is not an MP, and then demand that one of them resign to let the person take the safe seat and become an MP. It's totally wrong in my view.

"And then the person gets dictatorial powers in the House, with the members, by saying, 'If you don't vote *this* way you are out of the caucus.' It should be the caucus that decides whether the member is out, not the leader. And yet the leader can do it because they can say, 'I am not going to sign your paper—in the next election you're not eligible.' I would argue that should not be the case.

"It is something that has really gotten under my skin a bit about the way things have drifted," Milliken concludes. "In my view the party should be demanding some restriction on the powers of the leader, as part of their constitution, to make sure that we don't have this kind of dictatorship, really, arising—because the party leader becomes a dictator within the party. If he becomes prime minister, the powers are extraordinary—and that was not the way it was intended when we started our democracy in 1867."

Keith Martin is one of the few MPs who witnessed the exercising of the party leader's power on both the Conservative and Liberal sides of the House. An emergency room physician, he began his political career as a Reform MP in 1993 and then, when the Canadian Alliance amalgamated with the Progressive Conservatives, transferred his allegiance to the Liberal Party, serving there for another seven years, from 2004 to 2011. In his view, party policy is driven less by MPs responding to constituent needs and more by leaders, who are in turn pushed by pollsters. "It's poll-driven politics, and it's also driven by advisors, many of whom are quite young, highly radicalized, and driven by partisan interests as opposed to the public good," said Martin. "They have the power but don't have the responsibility or the accountability to the electorate. So they're severing [the relationship] between the elected officials and the public. The job of an MP now is to show up for the party, not for their constituents. . . . A lot of MPs feel disempowered."

Many former MPs' comments illustrated a conviction that the leader's tight control of their parties is stifling the propagation of creative solutions to legislative problems. But few expressed the idea with Martin's eloquence and forcefulness. He believes the leaders have consolidated control to the point that any expression of independent thought marks the idea holder as a potentially dangerous influence. "Even in doing positive things, [you] marginalize yourself because the leadership says, 'What the hell is he doing going off on landmines, or conflict prevention . . . or on Headstart programs for kids, or on Afghanistan—how dare he do that?'

"So the MP knows actually that if they start to innovate, they're marked down," Martin said. "The currency to success is to be able to do what you're told, and be partisan. And so, the MP is faced with a dilemma: innovate and represent your constituents on one hand, and on the other, you destroy your ability to advance. . . . The system works against innovation, works against independent thought, works against representing the constituents. When MPs are asked to [act according to] the public's expectation, the public's essentially asking them to do something that is going to be political harakiri within their own party. And MPs know that."

Like Milliken, Keith Martin believes the leader should not be empowered to decide who runs as a candidate in a given riding—because use of that power prevents the engagement of party members in the riding's political process. "Ridings have to be able to decide who their candidates are going to be," Martin says. "[Candidates] cannot be appointed from the leadership of the party. You have to engage the members of a party through a process that enables them to contribute to policies and things they'd like to see the party pursue, but there must be a feedback loop to the party. And caucus [must respond] to constituents. You're not going to do everything that they ask, but you need to have a transparent system where you're voicing the ideas that came in—'and here's what we've done with them.' So there's an accountability loop. We're not giving people any reason to join a political party."

Martin is also critical of a leader having influence over such appointments as who serves as whip, House leader, deputy House leader and other leadership positions in caucus: "They should be chosen by the caucus and not by the leader." He figures the public would be shocked if they discovered how undemocratic and punitive are the conditions imposed on MPs by the leader. The public, says Martin, "know something is deeply amiss in Parliament, and they think that MPs are there just to pad and line their pockets, they're full of power, they just are in it for themselves—which is not true. Most MPs, the vast majority, are not. . . . The way MPs and caucuses are managed is utterly toxic, by any measure of what good management practices are. . . . So, the management of caucus is done in such a way [as] to create a highly toxic environment that crimps and destroys the ability of caucus to work productively. And it's designed that way. Leaders choose to hobble their own caucus, but complain when caucus is not doing what they should be doing. It's just the management of caucus. Leaders need a course in management, basically."

SOME OF THE MPs we interviewed were less troubled by the power wielded by the party leader's office. Leaders have power, these MPs insist. But much of it does not get exercised in practice. Ed Broadbent acknowledged, for example, that as

NDP leader, he did have the power to hand-pick candidates who ran under the banner of his party. But he never did. "I strongly believe our constituencies—as long as we have our first-past-the-post system—the local constituency ought to be able to select their candidates democratically. The leadership of the party—nationally or provincially, or party executives outside the riding—should not have a role in it . . . it's just through public pressure that all the parties eventually, including the other parties, now get rid of this process where the leader can hand-pick a candidate and parachute him or her into the riding." It does not happen in the NDP, Broadbent said. "And I'm quite happy it doesn't."

We're accustomed to hearing about party whips and the application of party discipline from below, from the resentful people to whom it's applied. But Marlene Catterall, who served as the Liberals' whip and deputy whip, offers a different view of party discipline, one that reflects her conception of the job as more accommodating than most see it. "I always thought that my job was to make sure that, when legislation got to the House, any concerns about it among caucus members had been ironed out. And that often meant [making] substantial changes in the [proposed] legislation." Rather than the threats or any sense of the corporal punishment implied by the job title, Catterall portrays her "whipping" as more persuasive than punitive. Take, for instance, her anecdote about persuading fellow Liberal caucus members to pass legislation to protect Canada's endangered species.

The legislation was controversial. It embarrassed Canadian environmentalists that the United States had passed a law designed to protect endangered species in 1973. Yet

Canada's first real federal commitment along the same lines didn't come until nearly two decades later, with the Mulroney government's signing of the international Convention on Biological Diversity in 1992—which required federal passage of legislation. The next attempt followed after Jean Chrétien was elected as prime minister in 1993. The following year, the environment committee committed to enacting legislation, leading to the 1996 introduction of Bill C-65, an act "respecting the protection of wildlife species in Canada from extirpation or extinction." But environmentalists criticized the act as toothless; it protected migratory birds, fish and creatures on federal lands—and that was it. Certain creatures unlucky enough to have habitats on privately owned land were unprotected. And the process to incorporate new species into the legislation was seen as overly bureaucratic. The bill died with the 1997 federal election call, and stayed dead until Chrétien named David Anderson his environment minister in 1999. Anderson committed to enacting legislation designed to protect biological diversity. He tweaked the old Bill C-65 to ensure that it protected endangered species habitats regardless of whether they were on public or private land. The tweaks also bolstered the legislation's punitive power.

Still, there were holdouts. One of them was Charles Caccia, the Liberal chair of the Environment Committee. Anderson attempted to mollify Caccia and the other holdouts by describing the lengthy process that led to the act, the prolonged discussions, the negotiations, the balancing of this factor and that. One Parliament passed, then another, and still Caccia held up the legislation. Then his friend Marlene Catterall became whip in 2001. She talked to Anderson about what changes to the legislation he could accept in order to accommodate the likes of Caccia. Then she called Caccia into her office. "Charles," Catterall inquired, "tell me something: Is this legislation better than what we have now?"

"Yes, it is," Caccia said.

"Then why don't we pass it?"

"It's not as good as it could be," Caccia retorted.

"Charles," Catterall said, "I want to tell you that every time we write legislation it's an accommodation of a whole lot of different interests, especially in a country as diverse as ours. Consider this, Charles: The last time there was perfect legislation it came down the mountainside on two stone tablets, and it was dictated by God. And Charles? You are not God."

Then Catterall gathered Anderson, Caccia and the other Environment Committee Liberals, along with Chrétien's director of policy and research, Paul Genest. Neither side got everything it wanted, but the legislation was tweaked enough to allow both sides to vote for it, and it passed in June 2002. Catterall uses the point to illustrate the extent that "whipping" caucus can be less violent coercion and more glad-handing and gentle persuasion. Rather than a disciplinarian conveying edicts from on high in the leadership's office, Catterall portrays the whip as a conduit channelling information in both directions between the leadership and the caucus.

"It is a simple fact of life," she says. "If you have a hundred and eighty Members of Parliament, if every person was 100 percent satisfied with the details of every piece of legislation—as I said, we would have discussions about what goes into it, about how we're doing things, and if you had any group of people from across the country together, they would never agree entirely. And this country is about making those accommodations for our differences and for our diversity—it may be the most difficult country in the world in that way."

FEW MPS WERE AS accepting of the way leaders exerted power as Catterall or Broadbent. And for the less comfortable, it wasn't just the power of the party leader that was problematic; it was also the professional staff who worked close to the centre of power, whom Liberal MP Sue Barnes referred to as "this system of unelected people around the leader."

Time and time again, MPs from all parties lamented the amount of power exercised by the leader's office. Long-time MPs first elected in the Reform Party felt this acutely. "I think our democracy would be better served if parties were very principled and stuck to their principles. But the pursuit of power takes over the adherence to principles," said Conservative MP Brian Fitzpatrick.

"Look at the power—[the] prime minister can appoint every single judge, every single commissioner, every single . . . federal position. His office has the authority and power to do that," said Conservative MP Art Hanger. "I think they have too much power." As did several of his Reform Party colleagues, Hanger attributed the change to the moment his party shifted from reforming government to forming it. "People who had fought for and developed the Reform Association all of a sudden were part of the political machinery. They were no longer that grassroots push, as much. And then as time went on—after the first election—then you could see the change," he said.

Former Liberal MP Andrew Telegdi agreed—although Telegdi interpreted the cause through his own partisan lens.

"Harper . . . has everything going to the PMO, which means that the contribution that the other MPs can make is very seriously curtailed," said Telegdi. "That's the problem—and then it makes Members of Parliament redundant. So we have to make reforms because otherwise we are under-utilizing the Members of Parliament and alienating ourselves from the Canadian electorate." It was Telegdi who watched the early Reformers with admiration for their commitment to putting their constituents before their party. But that era has passed, he says: "Well, this has switched 180 degrees. . . . It's the nature of the beast. I mean to me, it's government wanting to control."

Finally, we'd be remiss if we didn't quote the rare present-day MP who, like his spiritual forebears in the Canadian Alliance, exhibited the courage to contradict his leader—Conservative MP Brent Rathgeber. "I joined the Reform/conservative movements because I thought we were somehow different, a band of Ottawa outsiders riding into town to clean the place up, promoting open government and accountability," Rathgeber blogged upon his resignation from the party in June 2013. Elected as MP in 2008 to represent the Alberta riding of Edmonton–St. Albert, Rathgeber was displeased when his party leaders edited his private member's bill. The original bill would have required the government to disclose any public sector salaries higher than $180,000. But in committee, Rathgeber's fellow Conservatives upped the salary level to $400,000, profoundly decreasing its potential effect. In protest, Rathgeber walked away from the Conservative Party. "Compliant MPs just do what they are told by PMO staffers. That the PMO operates so opaquely and routinely without supervision is an affront to the constitutional requirements of responsible government," Rathgeber continued online. "I barely recognize ourselves, and worse I fear that we have morphed into what we once mocked."

Centralization of power was a concern expressed by many sitting MPs—notably, all on the opposition benches—who responded to a project Samara initiated on the subject of redesigning Parliament. "The greatest challenges facing Parliament in the twenty-first century are the increased powers of the prime minister and the executive branch, and their refusal to permit Parliament to do its job of holding government to account," said Carolyn Bennett, Liberal MP for the Toronto riding of St. Paul's. Her colleague in the Liberal caucus, Vancouver Centre's Hedy Fry, expressed similar concerns that Parliament "is at risk of being redundant and irrelevant due to increased power in the hands of the executive."

IT HAS BECOME A FACT of business school case studies that technology tends to render irrelevant the middlemen who stand between suppliers and consumers. The process is called "disintermediation," and it's been bad for publishers and retailers in the book industry, and the record companies and retailers in the music industry. The same thing may well be under way now in politics, with MPs the ones to be disintermediated.

Early Canadian politics needed MPs. Sir John A. Macdonald needed members of his caucus—the likes of George-Étienne Cartier and Alexander Tilloch Galt—to assist with message dispersion and distribution, principally through speech making. But today, thanks to technological innovation, the MP's role as messenger is a far less important part of the job. Easy air travel means the leader can hop, skip and jump across this enormous country to personally rally the base and woo the electorate. Polling, communications technologies and mass media give the leader opportunities to listen to people's concerns—and convey back to them how the party is responding. Cementing the direct voter-to-leader relationships at MPs' expense is the reality of city newspapers, where most stories from Ottawa are syndicated nationally, with little local context or perspective. When it comes to national news, it's easier and cheaper to just follow Question Period than to chase down the local MP. Social networks make it easier for the leader to communicate with Canadians directly via a Twitter feed. MPs' relationships with constituents have suffered as a result, and pale next to citizens' sense of relationship with the party leader.

Strong organizations understand that these trends can translate into an empowerment of ground-level staffers. Think of how movements against drinking and driving, or climate change—even U.S. president Barack Obama—used these techniques to mobilize people. But not so in Canada—at least not yet. From what our MPs have told us, party leadership has too often responded to these trends by *disempowering* the intermediary, by treating individual MPs like "potted plants," "trained seals," or "bobbleheads," to say nothing of the dearth of opportunities for individual citizens to participate apart from the voting booth. Judging from the way they get treated, it would seem that MPs are regarded by their leaders as potential competitors for voters' attention. The clampdown on individual MPs ostensibly helps the leadership control the message and the party brand. Take Stephen Harper's government, whose individual MPs are required to submit their press releases for "vetting" through the PMO, according to Inky Mark. Whether you cite as evidence the Mark Warawa or Brent Rathgeber episodes, it seems clear that the Conservative political machinery frowns on anyone speaking out in any way that might be perceived to contradict the party platform—regardless of how their constituents may feel about the issue. The agency of the individual MP has diminished to a point where little remains at all.

This trend virtually extinguishes meaningful roles for MPs. It disengages voters from the MPs, the people best situated to represent their views to government in a meaningful way. And it discourages regular citizens from engaging in the political process: if they don't see an opportunity to have their voice heard by someone who understands and cares about the issues and attitudes where they live, why bother?

Reviewing the MPs' interviews, we feel our own mounting sense of frustration and regret. Why couldn't the MPs who complained in their exit interviews have pushed harder while in office to fix the problems they were complaining about now? Is it that the problems were only clear in hindsight? Perhaps the MPs hadn't been sure how to deal with them, or were consumed by more immediate priorities. Perhaps—and most likely—they too were victims of the tragedy of the commons—facing too many reasons not to speak up as they sat in Parliament and watched the slow degradation of our democracy.

An op-ed by former parliamentary budget officer Kevin Page in the *Toronto Star* drew attention to the book *Why Nations Fail* and its argument that nation-states tend to decline in proportion to the consolidation of political power in the country's leadership. In contrast, the book argues, nation-states tend to succeed in proportion to the dispersion of political power—in societies where a legislature holds government accountable. "Canada's Parliament is losing its capacity to hold the government to account," Page argues. "There are negative implications for prosperity and democracy. I am sorry if I sound brash, but we need to wake up. There is a lot at stake."

So: The result? Successive parliamentarians, over many decades, allowed the diminishment of their roles in favour of greater control by the party leadership. Now, for all parties, virtually every word an MP says in the House is scripted by the party leadership. Same with Question Period. Same with Members' Statements. Private members' business, where individual MPs were once free to vote as they wished, is now increasingly used by all parties to test prospective legislation. Any vote is regarded as a high-stakes test of party discipline—with the media pointing to differing opinions as leadership failures.

The silencing of debate and diversity of opinion described by the former MPs affects us all. It weakens our democratic institutions by making them less responsive to citizens and their representatives. It makes it more difficult to attract good people to public service. And it erodes Canadians' faith in their government.

Political journalist Andrew Coyne decries party leaders' accrual of power at the expense of individual MPs. "People like me are inclined to look for structural causes in cases like these," Coyne wrote in the *National Post*, referring to the Warawa affair but using language that could apply to any number of cases that saw the majority of MPs doing nothing while the leadership grasped for more power. "But it is as much about the character of the individuals involved. Because whatever the wishes of those in power, in fact everybody has a choice in these situations. The members of the committee who voted to throw out Warawa's motion knew they were doing a grubby, sordid thing. They did it anyway. The same choice awaited every other MP. They could, as few have done, stand up for what was right: they could protest against the leader's abuse of power and the steady erosion of MPs' prerogatives that made it possible. Or they could choose to pile on, and collude in their own servitude."

We'll conclude this chapter with a thought from the MP whose open dissent helped inspire other MPs to stand up against a leader they thought was moving their party in the wrong direction: Art Hanger, a principal actor in the Canadian Alliance coup against party leader Stockwell Day. Throughout his discussion with us, Hanger continually advocated for a measure that harkened back to his Reform Party days: greater freedom for MPs to debate issues as they saw fit, regardless of whether their opinions reflected the party's position, regardless of whether the opinions the MPs espoused were politically correct, regardless of whether the opinions were endorsed by the leadership. "I think that there should be more openness than what exists right now," Hanger said. "One of the frustrating issues for me, I think we should have a sound debate on a lot of things. . . . Why can't we have a debate on things that matter to our nation? Why not?"

Why not, indeed?

Toward a Better Politics

In 2009 we began our exit interviews in Samara's Toronto offices, out of concern for citizens' wavering interest in public life. Voting rates have been in decline for well over a generation, citizens see little value in public institutions and the gulf between politicians and those they represent grows ever wider. Perhaps optimistically, we anticipated that the people who had participated most directly in our nation's political life might have the best ideas about how to fix it.

The first MP we interviewed was the former Liberal member for Burlington, Paddy Torsney, who was first elected in 1993 at the age of thirty. Torsney told us the heartbreaking story of Christian Taylor, a seventeen-year-old boy in her riding who had died of anaphylactic shock after eating an apple turnover at a fast-food restaurant. The pastry contained hazelnut flavouring and Christian was allergic to nuts. After his death his mother, Betty Lou Taylor, began campaigning for a law that would require restaurants to post the ingredients used in their food. Torsney saw an opportunity to address a serious deficiency in food safety regulations and tried to present Betty Lou Taylor's proposed law as a private member's bill. Since the Liberal Party didn't pick up the cause and champion it (though several members defended it in the House), Torsney turned to others for support, but without the backing of her party, her bill ultimately died, as do so many other private member's bills.

Torsney's was the first of many stories we heard in which MPs stressed the value of working beyond their own party's stated agenda to advance issues important to them and their constituents. It was also the first indication our interviews gave us of the passion and determination that MPs bring to their work. Torsney remained in office for many years after her failed private member's bill, serving thirteen years in all, and she remains enthusiastic about this demanding and important work. "I think that it's just such an honour and privilege to be a Member of Parliament," she told us at the conclusion of her interview. "It's an amazing job and you can really affect people in big ways and in small ways if you use it for all the good things."

Again and again, in our exit interviews, we heard about former MPs' respect for the office itself. And yet, as the interviews progressed, despite ideological and geographical differences—whether the MP was from Toronto or Calgary, an urban or a rural riding, Conservative, Liberal, Bloquiste, NDP, Green or Independent—they all were concerned about how the MP's job was practised and perceived. Notwithstanding the pride they took in their service and what they were able to accomplish during their time on the Hill, they were deeply concerned about how Parliament functions, and especially the way party politics had come to dominate their lives.

At the end of every interview, we asked the former MPs how they thought Canada's democracy could be improved. What sort of advice would they give to parliamentarians who came after them? What might they change about the practice of politics to better serve Canadians? Their recommendations varied as much as their descriptions of their job. Only a few ideas were mentioned by more than five or six MPs, such as better MP orientation and training, improved civics education or eliminating Friday proceedings in the House of Commons (usually so they could get out of Ottawa and back to their ridings more easily).

Many of their recommendations amounted to mere tweaks in response to the broad concerns they had been describing to us—the bureaucratic failures that had forced them to intervene on behalf of constituents facing personal disaster; the challenges associated with simply engaging their constituents or building consensus on contentious issues. Proposed changes such as adopting electronic mechanisms to speed up House votes or giving greater authority to committee chairs are unlikely to put much of a dent in citizens' disaffection with their country's democratic process. Other recommendations bore little resemblance to those frequently debated in the media or in academic circles, or even to democratic reform proposals raised in various party platforms. Only a few MPs recommended institutional changes, such as Senate or party financing reform, for instance, and save for two former NDP MPs, no one recommended electoral reform or proportional representation.

As well as discussing changes to Parliament, the MPs were eager to discuss changes to the entity they felt created the real problems in Ottawa: their own political parties. The MPs wanted to see the centre of power move from the political party leadership back toward the MPs themselves. They wanted parties to exert less control over parliamentary functions such as Question Period and committees. It was telling that even the party leaders we interviewed proposed that this would be a good idea.

"Take a look at what the Brits do, where the first question is written and you get it ahead of time, so you are expected to give an intelligent answer," suggested former Liberal leader Paul Martin when describing how Question Period could be improved. Similarly, Martin thought committees should be made more effective: "Do not send substitute members who are on the committee to simply get your vote through. It's almost better that you just cancel the bloody committee. Respect that you're on a committee because you have developed an expertise, and let the committee function," he stressed.

But the suggestions were most often less specific, relating more to improving the conduct of public officials and their behaviour in the House. Recall Conservative MP Ken Epp's advice: "It's going to come from the leadership on top. I really would like to see party leaders from all parties engage in sober debate, and not throwing the malicious barbs back and forth."

Most of MPs' advice, however, centred more on survival as a Member of Parliament than on procedure or citizen engagement. Most commonly heard was the suggestion that incoming MPs "stay true" to their initial motivations, and not fall victim to the many small ways the political culture in Ottawa can force them to sacrifice their values. "Sometimes you get Ottawa-ized, and the next thing you're bringing your community the reasons why things can't be done as opposed to the reasons why things must be done. . . . Don't get Ottawa-ized. Stay true to what you believe in," said Conservative MP Randy White. In other words: don't become an insider.

Several descried the "Ottawa bubble," suggesting that the core work of the federal government was out of touch with the reality they, as outsiders, truly understood. "Don't lose sight of why you got into politics . . . public service. . . . . Don't get caught up in the Ottawa bubble, in the partisanship and the rhetoric," advised Gary Merasty, and "Be real. . . . Don't lose yourself in that infested water." Added Andrew Telegdi: "Don't sacrifice your principles in chasing after what [the party] can give you. Be true to yourself."

Torsney had similar advice: "Don't get caught up in what others are demanding," she said. "Be respectful of your colleagues . . . try to build friendships with colleagues across party lines. Understand their motivations, but understand what they can offer you."

IT'S CLEAR NOW that these exit interviews didn't offer up all the solutions that we hoped to find for what ails Canadian democracy. The former MPs were also at a loss for how to create a more effective culture in Ottawa and within their parties. Taken together, however, their narratives were full of advice. At the heart of the interviews was a collective *cri de coeur* for something bigger and more important than they could precisely describe on their own. Much as with the fable of the blind men and the elephant, where each feels and describes only one part—a tusk, an ear—without realizing that together they were describing the same bigger animal before them, as each MP shared his or her individual life in politics a clear, collective message rang through.

"The tragedy of the Commons is that public good is sacrificed on the altar of short-term political gain," observed

Reform-turned-Liberal MP Keith Martin. We discussed in our introduction the way the House of Commons reflects Garrett Hardin's concept of the tragedy of the commons—the way individuals, acting in their own self-interest, will conduct themselves in a manner that is harmful to the community's collective interest, and ultimately their own. As Martin realized, without an incentive to change, individuals carry on, depleting the shared possibilities for Canadian democracy with every passing day.

Canadians see the effects of this tragedy in the declining voter rates and the erosion of trust in governments. We see it in the difficulty parties have in finding people to run. We see it in Canadians' apathy toward Ottawa, and in the absence of respect for the occupation of politician.

We also saw it in the way the MPs spoke during their exit interviews, and the ways in which they, often unwittingly, reinforced the problem. We often witnessed a perplexing disconnect: strategic- and independent-thinking men and women who had apparently lost all sense of independence and initiative once subsumed under the party brand. They spoke of power residing elsewhere, and of politics as something that happened to them. We thought it remarkable that so many of these men and women, who had been elected by the citizens of Canada to represent their views to Parliament, would portray themselves as passive observers of a political process in which the party, or the leader, had become the primary agent.

The tragedy of the commons metaphor applies equally to political parties as it does to MPs. No party has an incentive to provide MPs with the autonomy they've surrendered over the decades. Nor does any individual MP have an incentive to risk the leader's censure by demanding more power. And so the tragedy persists.

"PEOPLE OFTEN ASK: How can we reform politics?" asked columnist Andrew Coyne at the start of the 41st Parliament. "And the answer is: we can't. There are very few institutional changes that would do any good, and whatever would has no chance of being enacted. We're not going to change politics until we change the culture." Coyne concludes his thought fatalistically: "And we're not going to change the culture."

We hope Coyne is wrong. And the route that hope might take is through the remaining agency of the individual MPs and the potential of what can happen when they express and marshal it. If one thing unites the eighty former parliamentarians who participated in our exit interviews, it was the belief that politics matters. Whatever the colour of their team sweater—red, blue, orange—no matter whether they favoured big or small government, a centralized or decentralized federation, every Member of Parliament we interviewed maintained that getting government right is critical to the way Canadians live together.

But if we're going to get government right, Canadians must believe that politics is worth their time, and more of us must actively participate. And for that to happen, MPs and political parties must change. This is a big job, but it has to start somewhere. Rather than wait for institutional or constitutional reform that would likely take years, if not decades, why not begin with things that can be done now? With things that signal that the principal players—MPs and their parties—are serious about the state of our politics and the low esteem in which Canadians hold our democratic institutions and those who hold office? And of course, journalists and citizens must create the conditions, and the pressure, for these players to change, and be willing to reinforce and support the people who make these overtures and demand something better. This will require a change in the way the media covers Parliament Hill. As former Conservative House Leader Jay Hill pointed out, it also would require that journalists and media outlets that cover politics not pounce on every caucus member who expresses an opinion that diverges from their party line, and not treat healthy exchanges of opinion in public as tantamount to treason or a pending leadership revolt. Citizens too must demand and reward a more nuanced political culture.

MPS, PARTIES, MEDIA and citizens, of course, simultaneously influence and are influenced by the others. There are messages in this book, however, for all of them. If one or even two begin to change, the others will find it easier. So who'll go first?

Let's start with parties. They represent something of a paradox in the Canadian political system: they appear to have few members, and very little legitimacy in the public eye. And yet, their influence in the public realm is immense and growing. Enabled by technology, social media and other direct communications technologies, and further aided by pollsters and a few slogans, parties are easily able to circumvent the connection between MPs and constituents. As power consolidates under the party leader and staff, MPs become increasingly powerless and the voters increasingly disenfranchised, making the misfortune of this behaviour all the more acute.

On reviewing the MPs' reflections, we came to understand that some of their aversion was well founded, exacerbated by political parties that had little respect for democratic processes or their very own members. For example, many MPs described the nomination as distasteful, opaque and unpredictable—though all of them, of course, had won their nomination battles. When the game's winners dispute how the game is played, it's probably time to be more clear about the rules. A well-run nomination battle can be one of the most inspiring events in politics, with the potential not only to transform the winner from citizen to politician but also to transform slightly interested citizens into engaged political participants. But the parties' apparent lack of concern for clean nominations reflects different priorities. At a bare minimum, parties should post clear nomination processes online to indicate how one goes about becoming a candidate, and how a citizen can get involved in the process. It may seem an obvious thing for parties to do, but in a review of over thirteen hundred riding association websites undertaken by Samara in 2013, fewer than 1 percent gave information about how to become a candidate. Just over 6 percent included the names of the local party executive team, and less than 5 percent had information on meeting schedules.

There is also a need for party leadership teams to improve the way they manage and lead in Parliament. The first priority is to convince parties to accord basic respect to MPs. What would that entail? Orientation procedures that assist new MPs in becoming productive more quickly after their arrival in Ottawa. Job descriptions clearly outlined and understood by the public, with responsibilities defined in a way that is conducive to feedback or recognition prior to the blunt review of the general election, and a culture in which achievement is tied to perceptible advancement. Leadership that encourages an understanding on the part of MPs of the need to focus their own energies where they can have the greatest effect. Rather than getting bogged down by direct involvement in individual bureaucratic manoeuvring, MPs could free up themselves and their staff to address the systemic problems their constituents are struggling with.

What else? One way to facilitate greater respect for the agency of MPs would be to require that they be allowed to serve out their full mandate in committee appointments. Greater tolerance for dissent would also make caucus more productive, since it would ease the pressure for consensus and allow better-informed policy to evolve from the wider diversity of views.

What can political parties do to reflect their role as the central vehicles through which citizens organize their politics? How can they act so as to encourage people to get involved? In order to build their legitimacy, and justify the tax subsidies they receive, they need to provide much more evidence that they operate openly, and that decision-making processes and accountabilities are clear—from the way they choose their candidates for election through to the way they design and approve advertisements. In short, parties should hold themselves to higher standards, and be held to higher standards by their memberships and by MPs themselves.

At a minimum, parties should conduct their business as transparently as we expect other public (and private) organizations to operate. They should report at least annually such basic data as the number of members and the number of donors (not just those over $200, as required by Elections Canada). Local party associations should also provide regular information on their activities, and how interested citizens might get involved. Parties should also make clear how much money they spend on the core areas of responsibility, including policy research and development, membership engagement, polling and advertising. Finally, parties should outline the decision-making processes for these key areas. Who, for instance, develops and authorizes their advertising campaigns? Why not require that negative ads be voiced over by the party leader, as Andrew Coyne has proposed, instead of some nefarious-sounding stranger? Or why not develop, as Susan Delacourt argues, standards for political advertising, or at minimum, require political parties to adhere to the code of Advertising Standards Canada, which forbids ads that attempt to demean or disparage? And when it comes to public policy, who decides what priorities should be pursued, and through what process? The purpose would not be not to prescribe dollar figures or the decisions that are ultimately made but merely to illuminate how they were made and with what considerations. While such openness would at first be uncomfortable to party insiders used to operating in backrooms, the status quo is untenable. In an era when citizens expect transparency, such important organizations cannot continue to operate in such hazy, mysterious ways.

Ultimately this may require the rules that govern parties and their way of conducting parliamentary business could include more sensible, articulate operating controls—the "mutual coercion" that Garrett Hardin describes. Parties are not constitutionally mandated but are privately constituted, citizen-directed organizations, not wholly dissimilar to other clubs or organizations. The difference, of course, is that they are the central vehicles through which politics is organized in Canada. They also happen to be among the most heavily tax-supported private organizations in the country, in recognition of their important public function. If political parties were to adapt to a newly mandated set of rules governing their operation, that funding could play as a key role in encouraging their compliance.

The historical record and common sense, not to mention Hardin's theory, suggest that these changes will be unlikely, absent any external impetus, such as pressure from party members and donors, citizens' groups or legal professionals. In a way, it is a surprise citizens haven't already called for greater scrutiny over the fuzzy ways political parties spend tax dollars.

Ultimately, however, changes in rules are unlikely to have their intended effect without a genuine realization on the part of MPs that democracy itself is at stake: that they, and their political parties, are approaching the point where citizens view them as nearly irrelevant. We need MPs to act as reliable, vibrant, two-way links between citizens and their government. At present, MPs have a long way to go. According to public opinion research Samara commissioned in 2012, Canadians give MPs failing grades in nearly every aspect of their work—from informing legislation to holding government to account. The research also indicates that Canadians believe MPs do a better job at representing the views of their party than representing their constituents. A report card so damning should spark MPs into action beyond asserting that they are different, and outsiders to the political status quo.

It was startling to hear how often MPs accepted their own helplessness, starting with the prevalence of the outsider narrative that so strongly permeated the MPs' reflections. Although there is beauty to be found in the MPs' stories of entrepreneurial success that we citizens don't hear much about or appreciate as we should, it's unfortunate to hear that most of these MPs—who worked in Parliament for, on average, over a decade, a third in Cabinet posts—still describe themselves as having felt power-less and outside the system. Why aren't these representatives of Canadians working within the system to make change? Or if they are, why aren't they willing to admit it?

It is time for MPs to confront, and change, the narratives they use to describe themselves. The myth of the outsider, riding into a town to save politics from itself, is a powerful one in our culture. Of course, the outsider narrative has been a part of poli-tics for generations; but still, it is ludicrous. Most MPs we inter-viewed weren't outsiders at all: most of them had participated in their communities as leaders in substantial ways. Several had worked hard as volunteers or paid staff for political parties, or as officials elected municipally or provincially. They had placed themselves in positions where they were certain to be asked to run. So why did they feel so obliged to wear the outsider cloak?

This is most likely because MPs know the public considers politics so distasteful that even long-time parlia-mentarians are reluctant to define themselves as a part of it. In this, the MPs agree with many Canadians: the way politics is practised is not particularly constructive or engaging. Even if the same MPs enjoy aspects of the political game—which is more likely, or else the games likely wouldn't persist—they also know that they turn people off politics.

But these narratives ring hollow in the ears of a cynical public. By distancing themselves from their chosen endeavour, explaining away their interest in public life and suggesting, for example, that their decisions to enter was a response to persuasion, the MPs set up a narrative that smacks of insincerity and perpetuates the problem.

Instead of claiming they didn't want to run, why didn't more say, "You know, I believe politics is a great way to make a contribution and I had my eyes open for a chance to participate?" This should not be a controversial statement, but from what the MPs told us, it would arouse suspicion about a candidate's motives.

The problem is made worse by the tendency to campaign, not just against a political opponent but against the occupation of politics itself. Of course, at a time when Canada is facing serious public challenges, we need elected officials who are willing to embrace their jobs, and describe why politics matters. Until we do, we should not be surprised that so few young people consider the political arena a worthwhile place to invest time or an effective way to make a difference.

MPs also need to better understand and stand up for their roles. Less than five of the eighty MPs we interviewed, for example, saw their role at all in terms of the traditional Westminster definition, centred on the MPs' task of holding the government to account. Instead, the MPs defined their jobs chiefly in terms of representing the views of constituents and those of the party, sometimes with specific reference to advancing legislation, although often in more vague, general terms. A subset of MPs emphasized solving constituents' problems with federal departments, such as Citizenship and Immigration Canada.

MPs are devoting substantial time and office resources acting as customer service representatives for the federal bureaucracy, thereby raising questions about bureaucratic accountability. But the impact of their efforts was more like plugging a single leak when the entire plumbing needs repair. If they are interested in processing immigration or veterans' claims, they should join the civil service.

They also failed to take responsibility for the impetuous behaviour on display in the House of Commons. Some even made a point of saying they never acted like those politicians we see on TV. "I set as a goal when I was elected to never heckle in the House and I hated when people banged their hands on the desk. I never once banged my hand on a desk. Not once," said Ken Epp, even after acknowledging that his own partisan behaviour had debased serious discussion on Canada's involvement in the war in Afghanistan. But there was a hall-of-mirrors effect listening to MPs disparage the rhetoric they heard in the Green Chamber: they spoke about it as if watching from the visitors' gallery, as if they hadn't in fact participated or, through their silence, tacitly endorsed the behaviour.

We acknowledge that party leadership pushes the MPs to issue catcalls and criticisms to help them define the party's position and frame their opponents in a bad light (though the impact of that rhetoric must be acknowledged—in what other workplace could any staff member so abuse a colleague or competitor?). "The party," however, was rarely personified or described. At moments, the exit interviews felt like something out of *The Wizard of Oz*, with the MPs expressing awe and fear of an ostensibly great and powerful figure behind a curtain, unknown and unnamed. While loyal to their leader, they displayed remarkable aversion toward leadership and those holding the reins of power—elected or otherwise. Most MPs were imprecise about who or what the term "party" described—as if not naming it dispensed them from dealing with it. Or perhaps it was a convenient way of ignoring the fact that those leaders were often people the MPs knew, likeable friends and colleagues. Or that the leaders might just be the MPs themselves.

Avoiding responsibility for the problems that plague life on the Hill was a constant in our interviews. MPs can blame the political parties. They can blame political staffers, their party leaders and the prime minister. They can blame the media and they can blame the culture of Ottawa. But at its root, any parliamentary problem exists because the Members of Parliament allow it to exist.

Should MPs so choose, changes could come very quickly, without legislative change or expensive consultation. Here's a start on a bucket list for willing MPs: refuse party-drafted talking points in the House and in committees; take steps to reaffirm a place between constituents and Ottawa; clearly articulate a job description and how to prioritize its key responsibilities. As a start, these measures will help clarify each MP's approach and enable citizens to know better what to expect from their elected representative.

There's more. Help localize the decisions made in Ottawa in a minimally partisan way. For example, following each Speech from the Throne, MPs should make a point of outlining what it means for their constituency, bringing their own voice and perspective to what may appear to be an otherwise distant presentation. Now that so few local news outlets have reporters in Ottawa, it is all the more important for MPs to provide that context if national politics are to remain relevant to their constituents.

And lastly, in the next election, each incumbent MP—as well as every candidate—should identify two or three pro-democracy commitments they'll make if elected. They could identify initiatives to raise voter turnout or advocate for greater transparency in their political party, starting with their local riding association. They could draft a code of conduct for themselves and their colleagues. They might even ask their constituents to suggest what changes they'd like to see that might lead them to hold MPs in greater esteem. Each of these steps, while small, can be easily accomplished and on a wide scale could achieve a powerful effect.

The MPs told us several stories about influencing legislation, such as policies aimed at renewing post-secondary education, when they banded together in small groups. Perhaps a similarly constituted group of MPs could work toward a movement for political renewal, and together slowly break through the tiring rhetoric that too often characterizes talk in Ottawa today. This could spark a much-needed discussion on the role of the MP in twenty-first-century democracy and how those roles should evolve so as to best serve the public.

There have been promising rumblings on Parliament Hill that suggest improvement is possible. We've seen backbench government MPs stand up to their leaders' efforts to silence them, and one, Michael Chong, go so far as to propose legislation on the matter. We've seen political parties promise open nominations, and an opposition leader include in his campaign promises the pledge to provide more power to individual MPs. Although he is far from the first to do this, maybe this time it will stick. We have seen veteran MPs realizing that they can articulate points of view that differ from those of their party, as they realize they don't always have to toe the party line. We hope to see more of all of this in future.

And while the primary responsibility for responding to the former MPs' appeal lies at the feet of MPs serving today, and those to come, they will ultimately act because we, the citizens, ask them to do so and support their efforts to make the changes our democracy so clearly needs.

The changes suggested in this book, in most cases, do not require complex legislative amendments. Although amendments to Canada's Elections Act or party constitutions may help move things along, in the meantime, let's not overlook small, basic changes that can take place tomorrow if the actors involved choose to make them a priority.

WHAT FORMER MPS told us about life in the House is not surprising. It's what most Canadians think every day. What is surprising is that it came from the MPs' mouths and with such consistency, regardless of their party or the region they represented. If we're smart we'll listen to what they said, even if we don't enjoy hearing it.

The MPs' successors have it in their power to demand changes and act differently, and the former MPs insisted that it is worthwhile to do so. As future crops of MPs enter the House of Commons, let's hope they'll act as Members of Parliament, and not just members of a party. And let's hope they'll resist the temptation to re-enact life on the kindergarten courtyard and come with ideas and initiatives of their own. Let's hope they advocate for reform within their own party.

Let's also hope that these new politicians will cease the toxic and counterproductive assertions that they aren't really politicians. If the newcomers really want to avoid being "typical politicians," then they should behave differently. They should embrace the politicians' role. They should take responsibility for the quality of politics and stop blaming an amorphous party. And when someone or something is to blame, they must call it out specifically, so it's clear who or what Canadians should hold to account, and what should change.

So let's finish with a look forward toward the careers of the 1,400 people who will be on the ballot in upcoming federal elections. We expect, at some point in future, that someone will conduct exit interviews with the MPs that rose from those hundreds of candidates. What will those interviews tell us? Whether those interviews happen in 2017, 2021 or 2025, we hope the political life of future MPs will have been something they planned and of which they were proud. We hope we hear people talk about what it was like being part of one of the best teams they'd ever been on. We hope we hear fewer tips on survival, and more stories of achievement. Perhaps more people will recall conversations like the one Paddy Torsney had with her mother, who, when Paddy decided to leave politics, said, "Now that you're not running, you can have a life." To which Paddy replied: "Mom, I had a life. It was a really good life."

We hope, in short, that our future MPs confront the tragedy in our Commons, and become the leaders our country deserves. It's in their hands, and it's in our hands—as citizens—to ask them to do so. If we don't, we are complicit in the tragedy.

Unless otherwise noted, MP quotations are from Samara's exit interviews. The list of the participating MPs is available at the end of this book.

INTRODUCTION

The public opinion research conducted by Samara can be found in Samara's publication entitled "Who's the Boss? Canadians' Views on Their Democracy," December 3, 2012, and is available at: http://www.samaracanada.com/what -we-do/current-research/who's-the-boss-.

The quote from Professor C.E.S. (Ned) Franks is from page 3 of *The Parliament of Canada*. Toronto: University of Toronto Press, 1987.

Garrett Hardin's essay, "The Tragedy of the Commons," was published in *Science*, New Series, vol. 162, no. 3859 (December 13, 1968), pages 1243–48.

The information on the pre-political backgrounds of elected officials was found in the article "There Was a Lawyer, an Engineer and a Politician . . .," published in *The Economist* on April 16, 2009.

The information on the candidates in the 2008 election was found in William Cross and Lisa Young's paper "Candidate Recruitment in Canadian Political Parties," presented by William Cross at a Canadian Study of Parliament Group conference on November 19, 2010, and is available at: http://www.studyparliament.ca/English/pdf/cross%20 pathstoparliament%20slides.pdf.

Data on Canadians' trust of various professions was found in two articles by Frank Graves: "The Trust Poll: Yes to teachers, no to bloggers," published on *iPolitics.ca*, May 13, 2013, and available at: http://www.ipolitics.ca/2013/05/13/the-trust-poll-yes-to-teachers-no-to-bloggers; and in "The Trust Deficit: What Does It Mean?," published on the *Ekos Politics* blog, May 13, 2013, and available at: http://www.ekospolitics.com/index. php/2013/05/the-trust-deficit-what-does-it-mean/; and in the article "Canada's Most Trusted Professions – 2012 Trust Poll Results," published in an undated article on the *Reader's Digest* website, and available at: http://www.readersdigest.ca /magazine/2013-trust-poll/canadas-most-trusted-professions -2012-trust-poll-results?id=3.

The speech by Michael Ignatieff, "On Partisanship: Enemies

and Adversaries in Politics," was based on a paper presented for the 2012–13 Stanford Presidential Lecture in the Humanities and Arts, Stanford Humanities Center, Stanford, California, on October 15, 2012. More information on the speech can be found here: http://library.stanford.edu/ blogs/stanford-libraries-blog/michael-ignatieff-presidential -lecture-partisanship-enemies-and.

The quote from Andrew Potter comes from his book *The Authenticity Hoax: How We Get Lost Finding Ourselves.* Toronto: McClelland & Stewart, 2010, page 196.

CHAPTER TWO

The quote is from Preston Manning's, *Think Big: Adventures in Life and Democracy.* Toronto: McClelland & Stewart, 2003. In addition to the account Solberg provided in his interviews with Samara, a major source of information for this chapter's opening anecdote is Preston Manning's written eyewitness account, originally intended for publication in *Think Big* and cut in that book's editing process. Manning graciously provided us with the unpublished account at our request.

The information on the election of independent candidates came from William Cross, "Candidate Nominations in Canada's Political Parties," chapter seven in Jon H. Pammett and Christopher Dornan, eds., 2006, *The Canadian Federal Election of 2006*, Toronto: Dundurn, 2006. The chapter is posted online at: http://paperroom.ipsa.org/app/webroot/papers/paper _5470.pdf.

Information on the history of political parties was found in "Registration of Federal Political Parties," Elections Canada, and available at: http://www.elections.ca/content.aspx?section=pol&dir=pol/bck&document=index&lang=e.

The information on leader-appointed candidates was found in Royce Koop and Amanda Bittner's paper "Parachuted into Parliament: Candidate Nomination, Appointed Candidates, and Legislative Roles in Canada," published in the *Journal of Elections, Public Opinion, and Parties* 21, no. 4, 2001, pages 431–52.

CHAPTER THREE

Information on the outcome of Gary Merasty's 2006 election was found in the article "Harrison concedes northern riding to Merasty," published in the *StarPhoenix* (Saskatoon), February 22, 2006.

The information on the popularity of the book *How to Be An MP* was found in Matthew Holehouse's article "How To Be An MP is the most borrowed book in Parliament," published in the *Telegraph* on February 12, 2013.

Barry Campbell's essay "Politics as Unusual: Darkness Visible" was published in the *Walrus*, April 2008.

The information on MPs' work-life balance was found in Royce Koop, James Farney and Alison Loat's article "Balancing Family and Work: Challenges Facing Canadian

MPs," published in the *Canadian Parliamentary Review*, spring 2013, pages 37–42. The book mentioned later, on the same point, is Steve Paikin's *The Dark Side: The Personal Price of a Political Life*, Toronto: Viking Canada, 2003.

Paul Szabo graciously provided us with a copy of his advice letter to new MPs.

Information on the government's handling of the apology to those in residential schools came from the following sources:

> Bill Curry and Karen Howlett, "Natives died in droves as Ottawa ignored warnings," the *Globe and Mail*, April 24, 2007. According to this story, the last residential school closed in 1996.

> "A Timeline of Residential Schools, the Truth and Reconciliation Commission," CBC News Canada, May 16, 2008, available at: http://www.cbc.ca/news/canada/story/2008/05/16/f-timeline-residential-schools.html.

> Canada, House of Commons Debates, 39th Parliament, 1st Session, Nov. 7, 2006 (Gary Merasty, Liberal), available at: http://www.parl.gc.ca/housepublications/publication.aspx?docid=2484588.

Additional information on Gary Merasty's retirement from politics was found in Jane Taber, "Dion loses a fifth Liberal MP," published in the *Globe and Mail*, July 12, 2007.

For more context on the role of an MP, see the Parliament of Canada, "On the Job with a Member of Parliament," http://www.parl.gc.ca/about/parliament/onthejobmp/index-e.asp. Also see Jack Stillborn, "The Roles of the Members of Parliament in Canada: Are They Changing?" (Ottawa: Library of Parliament, 2002).

Additional source material for this chapter was drawn from "Briefing Notes for New MPs," *Parliamentary Government* (February 2006), pages 17-20, and available at: http://www.parlcent.org/en/wp-content/uploads/2011/04/articles_and_papersParliamentary_Government_SpecialEditionFeb2006_EN.pdf.

Suzanne Dovi's article, "Political Representation," is from *The Stanford Encyclopedia of Philosophy* (winter 2011 edition), Edward N. Zalta (ed.), and is available at: http://plato.stanford.edu/archives/win2011/entries/political-representation.

John Godfrey's interview with *The Current*, CBC Radio, was held on September 14, 2011, and is available at: http://www.cbc.ca/thecurrent/episode/2011/09/14/constituent-services/index.html.

CHAPTER FIVE

Members' Statements were taken from Hansard, 40th Parliament, 2nd Session, May 29, 2009, and are available at:

http://www.parl.gc.ca/HousePublications/Publication
.aspx?DocId=3936180.

Paul Wells's comments on Question Period were taken from
"Stop the Madness," *Maclean's*, June 5, 2009, and are available at: http://www2.macleans.ca/2009/06/05/stop-the
-madness/.

The analysis of the discussion in the House of Commons
comes from the Samara report "Lost in Translation, or Just
Lost? Canadians' Priorities and the House of Commons,"
published by Samara on February 4, 2013, and available at:
http://www.samaracanada.com/docs/default-document
-library/samara_lostintranslation-pdf.

Andrew Coyne's suggestions for political advertisements were
drawn from his column "Attack ads are political deathstars
but their target is democracy," published in the *National Post*,
April 17, 2013.

CHAPTER SIX

Information on the size of Canada's federal debt in 1995 came
from Niels Veldhuis's report "Budget Blueprint: How Lessons
from Canada's 1995 Budget Can Be Applied Today," *Studies in
Budget & Tax Policy* (February 2011), Fraser Institute, page 11,
and available at: http://www.fraserinstitute.org/uploadedFiles
/fraser-ca/Content/research-news/research/publications
/BudgetBlueprint.pdf.

The cost of debt servicing came from Paul Martin's book *Hell or High Water: My Life in and out of Politics*, Toronto: McClelland & Stewart, 2008.

The editorial in the *Wall Street Journal* was titled "Bankrupt Canada?" and was published on January 12, 1995, and reprinted in the *Globe and Mail* on January 13, 1995, on page A21.

The impact of the 1995 budget on the size and spending of government was found in Anthony Wilson-Smith's article "Martin's 1995 Budget," originally published in *Maclean's* on March 13, 1995, and posted in *The Canadian Encyclopedia*: http://thecanadianencyclopedia.com/articles/macleans/martins-1995-budget.

Public opinion on the budget was taken from Peter Cook's article "The budget Canada needs, it also wants," published in the *Globe and Mail* on March 6, 1995, page B2.

Information on the finance committee recommendations came from John Geddes's article "Committee urges selected tax hikes," published in the *Financial Post* on December 9, 1994, page 3.

The *Wall Street Journal*'s reaction to Canada's 1995 budget was written in an unsigned editorial entitled "Canada Makes Right Turn," published on March 1, 1995, page A14.

The *La Presse* editorial cited was excerpted in André Picard's article "Quebecois Voices: The Answer Is Yes. What's the question? Commentators scoff at the PQ's referendum two-step," published in the *Globe and Mail* on March 2, 1995, page A23.

The *Globe and Mail*'s budget response was taken from the unsigned editorial "Budget-making politics," published on March 9, 1995, page A28.

The Fraser Institute's reaction to the budget was found in the report "Budget Blueprint: How Lessons from Canada's 1995 Budget Can Be Applied Today," cited above.

Information on House of Commons committees was taken from "Committees," from the *Compendium of House of Commons Procedure Online,* and available at: http://www.parl.gc.ca/About /House/Compendium/web-content/c_g_committees-e.htm.

The impact of federal-provincial transfer cuts on education was found in Roger Martin's article "Who Killed Canada's Education Advantage?," published in the *Walrus* on November 2009.

Jeffrey Simpson's assessment of Jean Chrétien came from Simpson's article "What He Leaves Behind," published in the *Globe and Mail* on November 1, 2003, page F10.

This chapter mentions two MPs who were not part of the exit interviews: John English and Alex Shephard.

CHAPTER SEVEN

An illuminating look at the tainted-blood controversy was found in Anne McIlroy and Edward Greenspon's article

"Blood crisis is Rock's test of fire: Golden boy of politics called heartless, cruel," published in the *Globe and Mail* on May 2, 1998, page A1.

The quote on Joe Comuzzi's commitment to the "traditional definition of marriage" came from Tim Naumetz's article "158 to 133: MPs approve gay marriage," published in the *Ottawa Citizen* on June 29, 2005, page A1.

Paul Martin's reaction to Joe Comuzzi's decision came from Terry Weber's article "Liberal steps down over same-sex bill," published in the *Globe and Mail* on June 28, 2005.

Bruce Garvey's quote on Joe Comuzzi's resignation came from Garvey's article "A hero among duds," published in the *National Post* on June 30, 2005, page A20.

James Travers's quote came from his article "At last, a brave politician acts with honour," published in the *Toronto Star* on June 30, 2005, page A31.

Information on the rarity of freshman MPs elected as Independents is found on page 3 of William Cross, "Candidate Nomination in Canada's Political Parties," a chapter in Jon H. Pammett and Christopher Dornan, eds. *The Canadian Federal Election of 2006* (Toronto: Dundurn, 2006).

The quotes from Leslie Seidle and Richard Simeon, as well as the comparison of Canadian and American party discipline, came from Gloria Galloway's article "Is Canada's party discipline the strictest in the world?," published in the *Globe and Mail* on February 7, 2013.

The "ladder of dissent" concept was first introduced in Samara's publication "It's My Party: Parliamentary Dysfunction Reconsidered," April 18, 2011, available at: http://www.samaracanada .com/Report3_Introduction. Jane Hilderman and Paul Thomas explored the concept more fully in a paper prepared for the 2013 annual meeting of the Canadian Political Science Association at the University of Victoria, "Climbing the ladder of dissent: Backbench influence in the Canadian House of Commons," available at: http://pauledwinjames.files.wordpress.com/2014/05/paul -thomas-cpsa2014v2.pdf.

Academic research on the impact of a local candidate on vote choice can be found in the article "Does the Local Candidate Matter? Candidate Effects in the Canadian Election of 2000," by André Blais, Elisabeth Gidengil, Agnieszka Dobrzynska, Neil Nevitte and Richard Nadeau and published in the *Canadian Journal of Political Science / Revue canadienne de science politique*, vol. 36, no. 3, July-August 2003, pages 657-664.

All poutine-related quotes and statistics were found in Peter Nowak's article "Poutine Wars: Cheese curds and gravy have gone mass market," published in the *Globe and Mail, Small Business* magazine on April 25, 2012, page 24.

Information on the "franchise bargain" of Canadian politics is available in the article by Roland Kenneth Carty, "The Politics of Tecumseh Corners: Canadian Political Parties as Franchise

Organizations," published in the *Canadian Journal of Political Science / Revue canadienne de science politique,* vol. 35, no. 4, December 2002, pages 723–45.

Information on the Elections Act and the public financing of political parties came from the following two articles, both published in *Money, Politics and Democracy: Canada's Party Finance Reforms,* edited by Lisa Young and Harold J. Jansen, and published by UBC Press in 2011:

> Harold J. Jansen and Lisa Young, "Cartels, Syndicates, and Coalitions." (chapter 1)

> F. Leslie Seidle, "Public Funding of Political Parties." (chapter 3).

Information on the survey undertaken by William Cross and Lisa Young is available in the article "Are Canadian Political Parties Empty Vessels? Membership, Engagement and Policy Capacity," published in *IRPP Choices,* June 2006, vol. 12, no. 4; and in the article "Policy Attitudes of Party Members in Canada: Evidence of Ideological Politics," published in the *Canadian Journal of Political Science / Revue canadienne de science politique,* vol. 35, no. 4, December 2002, pages 859-80. The survey was conducted in 2000.

Kenneth Carty's quote on Canadians' views on political parties was found in Carty's article "The Shifting Place of Political Parties In Canadian Public Life," published in *IRPP/ Choices,* June 2006, vol. 12, no. 4., page 5.

Information on Joe Comuzzi's decision to support the Conservative government's budget bill came from Gloria Galloway's article "Harper welcomes dissident Grit into the fold," published in the *Globe and Mail* on June 26, 2007.

Joe Comuzzi's comments on his departure from the Liberal caucus were found in Jane Taber's article "Dion drops Liberal MP for backing Tory budget," published in the *Globe and Mail* on March 22, 2007.

CHAPTER EIGHT

The cost of settling the defamation lawsuit against Stockwell Day came from Sheldon Alberts's article "'Leadership has exercised consistently bad judgment': MPs prepared to pay for breaking away from rank and file," published in the *National Post* on May 16, 2001, page A1.

Information on the undercover investigator hired to look into the affairs of Prime Minister Jean Chrétien came from Bob Remington and Joel-Denis Bellavance's article "Hold vote on leadership, analyst says: Day can't go on with disasters every week, professor says," published in the *National Post* on April 24, 2001, page A6.

Val Meredith's criticisms of Stockwell Day were quoted from Sheldon Alberts and Robert Fife's article "Day accuses rebels of betrayal," published in the *National Post* on May 15, 2001, page A1.

Chuck Strahl's comments at the May 15, 2001, press conference were taken from Sheldon Alberts's article "Leadership has exercised consistently bad judgment," published in the *National Post* on May 16, 2001, page A1.

Eoin O'Malley's research was found in his article "The Power of Prime Ministers: Results of an Expert Survey," published in the *International Political Science Review* 28, no. 1, 2007, and available at: http://dcu.ie/~omalle/070398_IPS_7-27.pdf.

The information on Sir John A. Macdonald's tenure was found in a *National Post* article by the historian Allan Levine, entitled "A brief history of Canada's parliamentary whips." Levine sources the "eighteen times" statistic to a 1985 study by Eugene Forsey and Graham Eglinton. The article appeared in the *National Post*, on April 3, 2013. A more thorough examination of Macdonld's life is available in two biographies by Richard Gwyn—*John A: The Man Who Made Us*, published by Random House Canada in 2007, and *Nation Maker: Sir John A. Macdonald: His Life, Our Times*, published by Random House Canada in 2011.

Information on the changes Pierre Trudeau made to his PMO were found in Bruce Wallace's article "Chrétien, a Closet Autocrat?," published in *Maclean's* on October 19, 1998, and available at: http://www.thecanadianencyclopedia.com/articles/macleans/chretien-a-closet-autocrat.

The quotes from Allan Levine on Pierre Trudeau came from Levine's *National Post* article cited earlier.

Jeffrey Simpson's book *The Friendly Dictatorship* was published by McClelland & Stewart in 2001.

For an in-depth look examples of and the wider context behind the centralization of power in Canadian government, see Donald Savoie's *Governing from the Centre: The Concentration of Power in Canadian Politics,* published by the University of Toronto Press in 1999, and *Whatever Happened to the Music Teacher?: How Government Decides and Why,* published by McGill-Queen's University Press in 2013. The quote from Chrétien's senior policy advisor is from page 89 of the latter book.

The quote from Gordon Robinson and the quote on the centralization of power in the PMO came from Elizabeth Thompson's article "PM's power threatens to make even Cabinet irrelevant," published in the *Montreal Gazette* on September 30, 2002, page A1.

Jeffrey Simpson's comments on the autocratic nature of the PMO came from Simpson's article "After the storm," published in the *Globe and Mail* on December 5, 2008.

Donald Savoie's quotes came from his book *Power: Where Is It?,* published by McGill-Queen's University Press, 2010, page 130.

Andrew Coyne's comments on Mark Warawa's 2013 motion, cited at two points in this chapter, came from Coyne's article "Mob rule versus Mark Warawa," published in the *National Post* on March 31, 2013.

Most of the colour here came from the Samara exit interviews. For a newspaper report that indicates the tortured history of Canada's endangered species legislation, see Kate Jaimet's article "Liberals demanded favours to pass bill," published in the *Ottawa Citizen* on December 27, 2002, page A1. Thank you also to Paul Genest for reviewing the account.

Brent Rathgeber comments came from his blog, entitled "I Stand Alone," published on June 6, 2013, and available at: http://brentrathgeber.ca/wordpress/i-stand-alone.

Kevin Page's article was called "Why being Canada's first parliamentary budget officer may have saved my life," and was published in the *Toronto Star* on April 1, 2013. The book he references, *Why Nations Fail: The Origins of Power, Prosperity, and Poverty*, was written by Daron Acemoglu and James Robinson and was published in New York by Crown Publishers in 2012.

CONCLUSION

The audit of political parties' riding association websites was conducted by Samara in the fall of 2013. Complete results are available at www.samaracanada.com/fun-stuff/riding -association-website-infographic.

Andrew Coyne's comments on changing the culture of politics came from his article "The people are what's wrong with our politics," published in the *Ottawa Citizen* on September 22, 2012, page A2. The reference to his suggestion that leaders voice-over negative advertisements was drawn from his column "Attack ads are political deathstars but their target is democracy," published in the *National Post*, April 17, 2013.

Susan Delacourt's book *Shopping for Votes*, published in 2013 by Douglas and McIntyre, is an invaluable resource in the evolution of Canadian political culture and contains practical suggestions for how advertising standards could prevent further deterioration of political discourse. These suggestions are elaborated further in her article "Political Reform: Let's overhaul the ad game while we're at it," published on December 6, 2013, in the *Toronto Star*.

The research on Canadians' views of their MPs is taken from the report "Who's the Boss? Canadians' Views on their Democracy," published by Samara on December 3, 2012, and available at: http://www.samaracanada.com/what-we-do/current-research/who's-the-boss-.

ACKNOWLEDGEMENTS

A project of this size and scope is not possible without the hard work, helpful advice and encouragement of a wide variety of people. We are particularly indebted to the generous support of the Canadian Association of Former Parliamentarians, and in particular to Léo Duguay, Francis LeBlanc, Jack Murta, Doug Rowland, Susan Simms and the late Honourable Douglas Frith, for supporting this project from its very early days, and to Jack Silverstone for continuing with that support.

Thank you also to the eighty former Members of Parliament, whose names are listed in the back of this book. They gave generously of their time and willingly shared their experiences and perspectives. We were told to expect reluctance on the part of many to participate in this project, and we were delighted to learn that this wasn't the case.

We are also grateful to those who worked with us to organize and conduct the interviews. Mariève Forest and Vincent Raynauld interviewed former MPs in French Canada. Reva Seth interviewed some of the MPs in southern Ontario, and Morris Chochla interviewed those in northern Ontario. Alison Loat and Michael MacMillan interviewed everyone else.

Peter McNelly provided interview training to ensure

consistency in the interviewers' approach. We are also indebted to Professor Mary Ann McColl for her training on qualitative research methods. Thank you to Ruth Ostrower, who coordinated the transportation and other logistics required to visit so many communities across Canada. Thank you also to Donna Banham, who transcribed the bulk of the interviews.

Thank you to Patrick Johnston for suggesting we get advice from former parliamentarians in the first place.

This project began with a series of short reports, published on Samara's website. This helped us identify the interviews' major themes and draw wider public attention to the MPs' experiences. Many people helped analyze transcripts and worked with us on these earlier summaries, including Heather Bastedo, Sarah Blanchard, Grant Burns, Suzanne Gallant, Shira Honig, Joshua Knelman, Andreas Krebs, Myna Kota and Elaine Lam.

Thank you to the team at Random House Canada for recognizing that there may be a book in all this, and in particular, to Brad Martin, Louise Dennys, Anne Collins and our tireless editor, Craig Pyette. Thank you also to copy editor Jane McWhinney and proof reader Liba Berry.

Samara's small and mighty team was critical to bringing this book to life. Kendall Anderson was involved from day one, helping to shape the initial proposal all the way through to providing invaluable comments on the final draft. Jennifer Phillips, Jane Hilderman and Laura Anthony brought their own substantial knowledge of politics to bear, providing comments, context and helping check critical facts, and with Leora Smith and John Beebe helped launch the book tour. Chris Shulgan's elegant prose brought the MPs' stories to life and helped make this book much more than we'd ever imagined. We feel very fortunate to work among such passionate, kind and thoughtful Canadians, and are so grateful for everything they've done to make this, and much of Samara's work, possible.

We'd also like to thank Samara's advisory and governance boards for their commitment to the organization, many since our initial days. Thank you to Sujit Choudhry, Heather Conway, Scott Gilmore, Kevin Lynch, Robert Prichard, Charles Sirois and Perry Spitznagel, and to Stephanie MacKendrick, Ratna Omidvar, Ruth Ostrower, Kasi Rao and Bill Young.

Our families have also been tremendously supportive to us during the founding of Samara and the writing of this book. Thank you to David Skok, Chris and Trish Loat, Cathy Spoel and Mary MacMillan.

As befitting a country with as large a geography and as diverse a population as Canada's, every MP's experience was in some ways unique, but we found they had more in common than we'd ever imagined at the outset of this project. We've done our best to tell their collective story and reflect their collective advice in the hopes that it reminds us all of the importance of public leadership and service to the well-being of our country. We encourage you to discuss and debate what the MPs have said, but please remember that any errors, of course, are our own.

Samara, the think tank we started in 2009 that has resulted in this book, is a charity and the proceeds from this book will go to support Samara's future work. Please visit www.samaracanada.com to learn more about what we do and how you can get involved.

PARTICIPATING MEMBERS OF PARLIAMENT

We wish to express our sincere appreciation to the former Members of Parliament who participated in this project:

The Honourable Peter Adams

The Honourable Reginald Alcock

Omar Alghabra

The Honourable David Anderson

The Honourable Jean Augustine

The Honourable Eleni Bakopanos

The Honourable Susan Barnes

Colleen Beaumier

Catherine Bell

Stéphane Bergeron

The Honourable Reverend
     William Blaikie

Alain Boire

Ken Boshcoff

The Honourable Don Boudria

The Honourable Claudette
     Bradshaw

The Honourable Edward
     Broadbent

Bonnie Brown

The Honourable Sarmite Bulte

The Honourable Rick Casson

Marlene Catterall

Roger Clavet

The Honourable Joseph Comuzzi

Guy Côté

The Honourable Roy Cullen

John Cummins

Odina Desrochers

The Honourable Paul DeVillers

The Honourable Claude Drouin

The Honourable John Efford

Ken Epp

Brian Fitzpatrick

Paul Forseth

Sébastien Gagnon

The Honourable Roger Gallaway

The Honourable John Godfrey

James Gouk

The Honourable Bill Graham

Raymond Gravel

Art Hanger

Jeremy Harrison

Luc Harvey

The Honourable Loyola Hearn

The Honourable Jay Hill

The Honourable Charles
    Hubbard

Dale Johnston

The Honourable Walt Lastewka

Derek Lee

Marcel Lussier

The Honourable Paul Macklin

Inky Mark

The Honourable Keith Martin

The Right Honourable Paul
    Martin

Bill Matthews

Alexa McDonough

The Honourable Anne McLellan

Serge Ménard

Gary Merasty

The Honourable Peter Milliken

The Honourable Andrew Mitchell

Pat O'Brien

Christian Ouellet

The Honourable Stephen Owen

The Honourable Denis Paradis

The Honourable Jim Peterson

The Honourable Pierre Pettigrew

Russ Powers

Penny Priddy

Jean-Yves Roy

Werner Schmidt

The Honourable Andy Scott

Bill Siksay

The Honourable Carol Skelton

The Honourable Monte Solberg

The Honourable Chuck Strahl

The Honourable Andrew Telegdi

Myron Thompson

The Honourable Paddy Torsney

Judy Wasylycia-Leis

Randy White

Blair Wilson

INDEX

last-minute speeches, 128

Leask, Bonnie, 58, 60

Lethbridge, 65

Liberal convention (1919), 195

Liberal-Conservative Party, 182

Library of Parliament, 80, 86

Loat, Alison, 72

local associations, 29, 44, 46–47, 226–27

London–Fanshawe, 53

Loubier, Yvan, 137

Louis-Hébert riding, 105

loyalty, 92, 159, 163, 164, 192

Lukiwski, Tom, 119–20

Lunn, Gary, 189

Lussier, Marcel, 96

Macdonald, Sir John A., 182, 194–95, 212

Macklin, Paul, 31, 69, 97

majority decision, 167

making a difference, 25, 30, 101–2, 113, 165, 171, 230

mandate letters, 180

Mandeville, Kathy, 40, 41

Manning, Preston, 39, 130, 170, 171, 189

Mark, Inky, 22, 47, 202, 214

Markham, 31

Markham–Whitchurch-Stouffville, 54

Martin, Alan Gray, 52

Martin, Keith, 120, 204–6, 221–22

Martin, Pat, 131

Martin, Paul, 8, 21, 49, 58, 75, 77, 79, 101, 136–37, 138–39, 148–49, 153, 156, 160, 162, 173, 177, 178, 187, 198, 220

Matane–Matapédia, 14–15

Matthews, Bill, 35, 167–69, 170, 182

Macdonald, Donald, 102, 104

McDonough, Alexa, 21–22, 91

McGuinty, David, 49

McKenna, Frank, 144

McLellan, Anne, 27–28, 34, 91

McNally, Grant, 189

McWhinney, Ted, 48

media

and party dissent, 165

blaming, 131

committee coverage, 142, 147–48

coverage of 1995 budget, 138–39

coverage of House Duty, 128

Question Period coverage,

Alison Loat is a regular commentator on Canadian politics, a graduate of the Harvard Kennedy School of Government and a former consultant with McKinsey & Company. For her work as a co-founder of Canada25, she was recognized as a young leader by *Maclean's* and the Public Policy Forum. She was also selected as one of the top 100 women in Canada by the Women's Executive Network, and received both the Gold and Diamond Jubilee Medals for her service to Canada. Alison is also an associate fellow and instructor at the School of Public Policy and Governance at the University of Toronto. Follow her on Twitter @AlisonLoat.

Michael MacMillan is the CEO of the Canadian-based company Blue Ant Media. He was previously the executive chairman and CEO of Alliance Atlantis Communications. MacMillan co-founded the original Atlantis Films in 1978, which won an Oscar in 1984 for its short film *Boys and Girls*. A recipient of the Gold and Diamond Jubilee Medals for service to Canada, he is also a co-owner of Closson Chase, a vineyard and winery in Prince Edward County, Ontario.

Alison Loat and **Michael MacMillan** co-founded the think tank Samara in 2009 (www.samaracanada.com). Follow Samara on Twitter @SamaraCDA.